WHAT WE
DON'T GET
ABOUT GOD
& GRACE

Charleston, SC
www.PalmettoPublishing.com

What We Don't GET about God & GRACE
Copyright © 2023 by W. F. Hauck

Hardcover ISBN: 979-8-8229-2602-8
Paperback ISBN: 979-8-8229-2603-5
eBook ISBN: 979-8-8229-2604-2

WHAT WE DON'T GET ABOUT GOD & GRACE

THE MYTH OF ORIGINAL SIN & OUR "FALL" FROM GRACE

W. F. HAUCK

TABLE OF CONTENTS

INTRODUCTION

"William, your penchant for heresy will see you in Hell!" Ever been told you deserve to go to Hell? And not by your drinking buddies after a particularly disgusting joke, either. Well, I have… several times… and by my (former) minister no less! Usually that proclamation was closely followed by, 'The Bible clearly says!" Well, those of you who choose to continue reading my interpretation of where Christianity has missed a switch point and jumped the track might end up joining the chorus. However, I adjure you to read on and, at least, consider what I am suggesting. You may very well come to find hope for all humanity, and I mean ALL!

Let's go back to that initial assertion; "the Bible clearly says!" I clearly challenge such a concept. The

Bible is a collection of ancient writings which grew, in many cases, from oral traditions transcribed into ancient languages from which they were hand copied through the centuries from Aramaic to Greek, Latin, to forbidden tomes of King James era English until finding their way into Southern Baptist fire and brimstone. What could go wrong? In at least one of these jumps of faith the old excuse, "It's Greek to me," comes into play. Even our common concept of **Hell** is derived from three independent root words, the most common of which, hades, simply refers to the grave or even a simple hole. **Love** itself comes from as many as five.

"But, but, but…" I can hear the chorus of many, "the Bible is revered as God's infallible words … isn't it?" Every single word?   Even conjunctions? How about punctuation and vowels, which Hebrew presumes rather than includes when written? Well, just to get the show under way, I offer up one profound question: Why does Christianity celebrate Easter on two different days? Western Easter was observed this year on April 9th but Orthodox (Greek Easter) was scheduled for April16th? I know, I know, it's Greek to me; but you'd think God would see that something so vital to Christianity would be plainly set forth.

Well at least they both have the Resurrection penciled in on a Sunday. Oh, wait, that's another issue, that **sign of Jonah** problem I'll circle around to later. For now, let's focus on how the book was put together... three centuries after Jesus Christ brought His Gospel of the future Kingdom of God.

Are you familiar with Emperor Constantine of Rome? How about the Nicene Creed? OK, I see a lot of hands raised. That being the case, how many of you know how to connect the two? Here's a hint: The Council of Nicaea was held at Constantine's, palace overlooking Lake Nicaea. Are y'all beginning to hear my point steaming 'round the bend? Here's the rest of the story.

The Empire was in trouble. The followers of numerous pagan deities were causing serious schisms and the barbarians were smelling blood. Constantine was desperate for a means to unify the empire. The obscure Jesus sect derisively referred to as Christians had recently come out of severe persecution and was gaining in popularity. The new emperor decided that declaring Christianity, with its iconic deity, as the new state religion could solve the problem. However, reports from Alexandria of dissension amongst the faithful, the **Arian Controversy**, over the nature of Jesus was leading to actual bloodshed. Something had to be done to provide unity.

Imagine that; hundreds of years after the sacrifice of Jesus, His church was still divided over whether He had been divinely born as God in the Flesh or a fleshly human avatar within whom God dwelt... and they were shedding their own blood over it! That's almost as stupid a fighting over whether a biological male can give birth. I'll circle back to those details in a later chapter, as well.

Constantine, who preferred the avatar of a god dwelling amongst us as a man to lead the empire, probably conceived of how such a deity could also assume the same role as emperor. Obviously, his guidance was needed in the here and now. So the ruler of the future Holy Roman Empire arranged for leaders of this new religion to be invited to the First Council of Nicaea where "rules of engagement would be determined.

It was obvious a rulebook needed to be agreed upon. Jewish scriptures from the Greek Septuagint would be included with newer testimonial writings about Jesus into what would become The Bible. Another council was selected to vote upon what would and wouldn't be accepted into the Holy Canon. In Alexandria alone, there had been more than 120 Gospel accounts of the life and message of Jesus. Anything not accepted was to be burned. Anyone possessing unauthorized scriptures would be subject to execution. There were, as you know, merely four included.

But wait, there's more! This Bible was not meant for the masses. It was to be for the exclusive use of those leading the Masses. Not only was it too costly for the average person, if he could read at all, it was also hand written in Latin. Martin Luther and William Tyndale are the men we have to thank for translating the Latin scriptures into modern language. William Tyndale was even burned at the stake as a heretic for creating the King James Bible. We have heretics and Guttenberg to thank for our freedom to read and worship God as we feel inspired to so do.

From this mélange we get all the varied versions of the "inerrant word" of God. But as dear old Pappy used to say, "If'n dat ole King James version twas good 'nuff f'Jesus, tis good 'nuff f'me!"

Hope y'all still be with me.

CHAPTER ONE

FAITH AT THE CROSSROADS

This is for those whose faith has been compromised by society, science, and just about anything thrown our way by what passes in our lives as reality. It is not directed at those blessed few who never doubt their faith. If you prefer to believe creation occurred some 6000 years ago, I have no problem with that. What really matters is how Jesus affects the way in which you treat others. I have no desire to weaken the faith of any one within whom doubt has no home; unless, that is, you'd like to learn how to solidly refute all those doubts cast by scientific observation and smart-ass relatives. I was once, after all, included within that population. I now find understanding such translations further strengthens my faith.

Then, one magic day, circumstance shook my "stable world". I took notice that the weekly calendar began on a Sunday. That confused my teenaged presumptions. When I questioned it I was informed that, yes, Sunday is the first day of the week. When I asked why we observed the first day of the week instead of the seventh, I was admonished not to trouble my "little" mind about it.

"I believe, Father, help my unbelief!" became the mantra that eventually led, 60 years later, to this book; a study that answers the Sunday question as well as so many others. As a result, I no longer suffer such doubts…about God, that is. However, regarding those who proclaim, "the Bible clearly says?" Not so much. Let's begin with a **Passover Seder** otherwise known as the **Last Supper**.

Jesus had gathered his disciples together to celebrate the holy observation we often see represented in a "photo taken" centuries later by *Leonardo DaVinci*, to prepare them for what was to come. The record of that event is pretty accurate, except there were more than The Twelve in attendance. After Jesus instituted the Eucharist's allegorical consumption of Christ's blood and flesh, many were offended by the less-than Kosher symbology and left. Keep in mind Jesus was still expected to lead a rebellion. That's the real reason for Judas's 'betrayal.' He believed doing so would force Jesus to take action. Why else would Judas have hung himself when it all went south on him?

Before pushing off, let's reacquaint ourselves with the spirit in which Jesus created His "little flock." One of the final lessons Jesus conveyed to His disciples occurred in the midst of a meal, suggested by many commentators to be at the Last Supper. God will it to be so in our lives.

John 13:2-5 The evening meal was being served, and the devil had already prompted Judas Iscariot, son of Simon, to betray Jesus. Jesus knew His Heavenly Father had put all things under his power, and that he had come from God and was returning to God; so, He got up from the meal, took off his outer clothing, and wrapped a towel around his waist. After that, he poured water into a basin and began to wash his disciples' feet, drying them with the towel that was wrapped around him. NIV

Matthew Henry's Commentary illustrates why Jesus came to fishermen instead of religious leaders, explaining His extraordinary action as follows:

(1) The action itself was mean and servile, and that in which servants of the lowest rank were employed. Let thine handmaid (saith Abigail) be a servant to wash the feet of the servants of my lord; let me be in the meanest employment, 1 Sam 25:41. If he had washed their hands or faces, it had been great condescension (Elisha poured water on the hands of Elijah, 2 Kings 3:11); but for Christ to stoop to such a piece of drudgery as this may well excite our admiration. Thus, he would teach us to think nothing below us wherein we may be serviceable to God's glory and the good of our brethren.

(4) He put himself into the garb of a servant, to do it: he laid aside his loose and upper garments, that he might apply himself to this service more expeditiously. We must address ourselves to duty as those that are resolved not to take state, but to take pains; we must divest ourselves of everything that would either feed our pride or hang in our way and hinder us in what we have to do, must gird up the loins of our mind, as those that in earnest buckle to business.

(Matthew Henry's Commentary on the Whole Bible: New Modern Edition, Electronic Database. Copyright (c) 1991 by Hendrickson Publishers, Inc.)

John 13:12-17 When he had finished washing their feet, he put on his clothes and returned to his place. "Do you understand what I have done for you?" he asked them. "You call me `Teacher' and `Lord,' and rightly so, for that is what I am. Now that I, your Lord and Teacher, have washed your feet, you also should wash one another's feet. I have set you an example that you should do as I have done for you. I tell you the truth, no servant is greater than his master, nor is a messenger greater than the one who sent him. Now that you know these things, you will be blessed if you do them. NIV

Luke 22:24-30 a dispute arose among them as to which of them was considered to be greatest. Jesus said to them, "The kings of the Gentiles lord it over them; and those who exercise authority over them call themselves Benefactors. But you are not to be like that. Instead, the greatest among you should be like the youngest, and the one who rules like the one who serves. For who is greater, the one who is at the table or the one who serves? Is it not the one who is at the table? But I am among you as one who serves.

Here is an example to us all: "Whoever desires to save his life will lose it, but whoever loses his life for My sake will save it." This is why He also said it is easier for a camel to pass through the Eye of the Needle (the narrowest gate into Jerusalem where at camels had to be unloaded before squeezing through) than for a rich man to enter the Kingdom of God. Those of us with little to lose are more than willing to risk our widow's mite for "the cause." Once risen to success, however, we tend to be much too fearful of losing those false riches to risk for the sake of conscience. It is a fact of life that trials strengthen us while success tends toward the opposite. There was a point in history when the Church stood at just such a crossroads. On our continuing journey down this stream of discovery which path was chosen will quickly become apparent.

As a final example of something to keep in mind as we discuss the treatment accorded to heretics as being apostates consider Peter's denial of Jesus in His hour of need.

> Luke 22:31"Simon, Simon, Satan desires to sift you as wheat. 32But I have prayed for you, Simon, that your faith may not fail. And when you have back, strengthen your brothers."
>
> 33But he replied, "Lord, I am ready to go with you to prison and to death."

34Jesus answered, "I tell you, Peter, before the rooster crows today, you will deny three times that you know me."

Luke 22:54-62 Then seizing him, they led him away and took him into the house of the high priest. Peter followed at a distance. But when they had kindled a fire in the middle of the courtyard and had sat down together, Peter sat down with them. A servant girl saw him seated there in the firelight. She looked closely at him and said, "This man was with him."

But he denied it. "Woman, I don't know him," he said.

A little later someone else saw him and said, "You also are one of them."

"Man, I am not!" Peter replied.

About an hour later another asserted, "Certainly this fellow was with him, for he is a Galilean."

Peter replied, "Man, I don't know what you're talking about!" Just as he was speaking, the rooster crowed. The Lord turned and looked straight at Peter. Then Peter remembered the word the Lord had spoken to him: "Before the rooster crows

today, you will disown me three times." And he
went outside and wept bitterly. NIV

Yet, Jesus forgave Peter his apostasy and made him
head apostle; indeed, many feel Jesus said Petros was
the rock upon which He would establish His church.
Either way, the humble and servile manner in which
Jesus instructed and led His disciples, teaching them to
do the same, is hardly the manner in which the church
behaved as Jesus was gradually turned from example
to idol. There is no better time to begin this than that
moment in history when the church began to morph
from persecuted to persecutor. That adulterous step
from ministerium to dominion, from humility to pre-
sumption, when the priestly order replaced by Jesus
managed to return the favor and regain control. of
the sanctuary.

Jumping forward some three centuries in time to a
point where the fledgling church of Jesus has emerged
from the great Roman persecution, Rome is suffering
an identity crisis. Two religious' leaders in Alexandria,
Bishop Athanasius and a priest named Arius have
faced off in an, often, violent dispute over the essence
of Jesus the Christ…yes, whether He was God in the
flesh, or a divinely inspired human within whom God's

Holy Spirit had taken up residence. Imagine that; three centuries later, that issue was still worth fighting over. The "brethren" of Jesus were actually resorting to bloodshed! And we wonder at the schisms within the Christian faith some two thousand years after the fact.

At the same (hysterical) historical moment, Emperor Constantine of Rome was struggling with issues of social decay within the empire. The Roman society had become hopelessly fragmented amongst numerous pagan gods. He had, with the help of Bishop Hosius, conceived of a plan with which to unite the disintegrating social structure under a single deity. The new Jesus Movement, with its single divine entity seemed to hold great promise. But first, the internecine fighting amongst the faithful had to be dealt with and a comprehensive "rule book" assembled. Prior to sending out invitations to Christian leaders to assemble at his private villa located on the shores of Lake Nicaea, Constantine sent his personal mole, "Bishop" Hosius, to report back on how to deal with the strife in Alexandria. By now many of you have figured out where this is headed.

What a sight the, seemingly, endless stream of Christian officials arriving at the 1st Council of Nicaea must have been! Many of the dignitaries were crippled limping along minus various limbs, some missing eyes and ears and baring other scars earned for their resistance to the edicts of Rome during the recently ended Great Persecution. "This must seem like their savior has returned for them," Bishop Hosius probably proclaimed as he joined his host, Constantine. For certain, they must be convinced the Kingdom of Heaven is now at hand."

"Arise and come forth, mi ami," Constantine had likely declared as Hosius arrived. "All others leave my presence immediately," he further gave command. Without hesitation, the guards and personal attendants backed their way out of the chamber. At the further behest of Constantine, the Praetorian Guards closed the great doors, and Constantine bounded from his throne to close the distance between them. His face was quickly transformed from its previous stern expression to a broad and easy smile.

"Hosius, my great friend," Constantine declared as the two clasped hands to shoulders. "How good it is to see you again – and looking so hale and hearty. How was the journey? I trust your crossing was not a difficult one?"

"Tiring as always, my Lord. But we were blessed with favorable winds to shorten our ordeal. We made proper sacrifice to both Poseidon and Neptune just to be sure one did not feel slighted."

"Indeed, mi ami. The seas are treacherous enough without offending a resident deity. I so prefer the land to the unknown depths, even if it is much slower. Besides, it is never good for my subjects to see their personal demi-god casting his accounts over the rail," he added while miming sea sickness. "Best to reserve such behavior to the privacy of a proper vomitorium." To that, they likely erupted into mutual hilarity at some private joke or experience. One can only imagine.

"Now," Constantine probably asked as he led the way off to lounge on a set of couches. "What news do you bring of the strife in Alexandria?"

"Both good and bad, I must report, Your Majesty. However," Hosius added as Constantine's face took on a troubled look, "the bad will be tempered by the good if we play our cards right."

"Continue," Constantine commanded.

"First off, I met with Bishop Alexander and sympathized with him as a fellow Bishop myself. I made it plain that the escalation of conflict amongst high-ranking Christians was not only disruptive of Church unity, but disreputable and almost certainly unnecessary as all Pagans openly taunted such argumentative fools who might think themselves representatives of the one true God. How, in God's name, could such potential be allowed to risk fracture by squabbling theologians?

"Why, I asked him, put all this at risk by fighting over abstract technical questions which none could answer with certainty. The differences between "begotten" or "created," and "divine by nature" or "divine by adoption" were essentially trivial. Those who presumed to represent Christ should learn from the Greek philosophers who had dealt with disagreements far more profound than this without calling each other devils or organizing factions to suppress each other's opinions. The adversaries should reconcile and permit the emperor to once again, enjoy 'trouble free days and nights of repose.'"

"And, I assume by the tone of your report, that he was less than cooperative?"

"Indeed, he expressed regret that you, his emperor, should be suffering sleepless nights over this. But could we not see how pernicious the Arian doctrine was -- how blasphemous to Christ and the Church?' Of course, we could not be expected to understand such complex theological issues. We are, as he foolishly asserted, Latin speakers unfamiliar with the subtleties of Greek thought. But surely, we should recognize rebellion when we see it. 'The refusal of Arius to recant his heretical viewpoint, his plots with other churchmen to overthrow the decision of his bishop, the arrogant tone of his letters, were all proof of his utter disregard for the principles of order so valued by you,' my Lord.

"Finally, he asserted that since his jurisdiction included all of Egypt from the world's most populous city to the rich farmlands that supplied most of Rome's grain, the towns and cities of the Nile valley and the monasteries of the Theban and Nubian deserts as well as Libya from the "Five Cities" of the urbanized north to the African desert, he was foremost Papa among all other bishops. 'If a church council were needed, HE would convene it.' No doubt its conclusions would most certainly reflect his own views."

"This is the good news?" Constantine roared. "While I can admire a man with as much gall as I possess, I cannot coexist with him. He must be destroyed before we can move forward!"

"With all due respect, my Lord. It would be better to use his authoritarian attitude to our advantage – to rid ourselves of all other potential competition – THEN, deal with him at the proper moment."

Constantine settled back in contemplation. Then raised a question. "But if he ignores our council – as he has hinted at doing in favor of hosting his own…?"

"As powerful as he may think himself, he is but one man. His ranks are rife with dissension. Only you command and conquer. Knowing that, he will fear that Arius might gain the upper hand with you – especially should you seem to favor the priest. That is the hand we must play against him – the winning hand, my Lord and Emperor."

Constantine smiled once again. "First, we drink. Then, we plan."

"That is exactly why we shall prevail. Come, let us prepare for your grand entrance, my Lord."

CHAPTER TWO

HOW THE BIBLE WAS ASSEMBLED

Contrary to popular folklore, the Christian Bible wasn't handed to the disciples by Jesus as a going away present, although I have found most believers don't actually think about that much less get the significance of it. So, then, just what do we know about it? How many of us are aware of how the collection of writings we know as the Holy Canon was assembled? I know I wasn't originally. The process of deciding (by committee) what should or shouldn't **be included didn't** begin until after the 4th century. Nicaea Council. To study how Constantine's 'select committees' went about it would be much like watching sausage being made as the old saying goes. "Well, then," you might ask, "If there was no Bible available during "Bible Times," just what did the early church use as a guide?"

In his second Epistle to Timothy, Paul asserts in (2 Tim 3:14-15) "...for from your youth you have known the scriptures from which you are able to be wise unto salvation." Really? Since this epistle of Paul was yet to become part of the Bible, what scriptures might Timothy have been aware of <u>from the days of his youth?</u> See, it's simple little things like this that most readers quickly pass over without alarm bells sounding. Obviously, Paul was referring to the Old Testament **Septuagint**: the prophetic Jewish scriptures translated into Greek in the 3rd century B.C. It's from these which the Bible's Old Testament was to be compiled. What we consider the New Testament (mostly letters written to the various newly formed church congregations and certain individuals) , had yet to be compiled. Some of the "books of the Bible like St. John's **Apocalypse**, were yet to be written.

That project became the focus of Constantine's new organization, although the final agreement as to the biblical canon was not agreed upon till the fifth century.

Emperor Constantine had taken a personal interest in several ecumenical issues in 316, and he wanted to bring an end to the *Christological dispute.* To this end, he sent Bishop Hosius of Cordoba to investigate and, if possible, resolve the controversy. Hosius was armed with an open letter from the emperor to wit: "Wherefore let each one of you, showing consideration for each other, listen to the impartial exhortation of your fellow-servant." However, as the debate continued to rage despite all efforts of the Bishop, Constantine, decided to resolve the issue one way or the other. Which it would be didn't really matter so long as the arguing ceased. Therefore, he called for a gathering of church leaders from all parts of the empire to resolve this issue at his Villa on the shores of Lake Nicaea. The council was presided over by the emperor himself, who participated in and even led some of its discussions.

At this First Council of Nicaea 22 bishops, led by Eusebius of Nicomedia, came as supporters of Arius. Still, when some of Arius's writings were read aloud, they were denounced as blasphemous by most. Those who upheld the notion that Christ was co-eternal and consubstantial with the Father were led by Bishop Alexander's defense that the Son was one in essence with & eternally generated from the ***ouisia*** of the Father.] Those who instead insisted that the Son of God came after God the Father in time and substance were led by Arius the presbyter.

For about two months, apparently having never been instructed by their parents to avoid discussing politics and religion, they set off to do both. The two sides argued and debated, with each appealing to Scripture to justify their respective positions. Bishop Alexander proclaimed the position of Athanasius that the Son was of the same essence (ouisia) of God the Father, hence also God in the fleshly form of Jesus. Against this, maintaining God the Father alone was infinite and eternal, Arius countered that opinion.

"Since the Son was directly created and begotten of God, there had to have been a time when he had no existence. Hence He was a finite being." Arius appealing to Scripture, quoted John 14:28: "the father is greater than I" as well as Colossians 1:15: "the firstborn of all creation." Thusly, Arius insisted the Father's divine essence was greater than the Son's, and that the Son was under God the Father, and not co-equal or co-eternal with him. Of such silly arguments are the ways in which Jesus was reduced to non-effect. Mis-quoting Hillary, "At this point what difference does it make?" Today we might best refer to Him as God's Avatar.

According to some accounts debate became so heated that Bishop Nicholas struck Arius across the face. The majority of the bishops ultimately agreed upon a creed, known thereafter as *the Nicene Creed*. It included the Greek *homoousios*, meaning "consubstantial", or "one in essence", which was incompatible with Arius's beliefs. On June 19, 325, council and emperor issued a circular to the churches in and around Alexandria: Arius and two of his unyielding partisans (Theonas and Secundus)] were deposed and exiled while three other supporters—Theognis of Nicaea, Eusebius of Nicomedia, and Maris of Chalcedon— affixed their signatures solely out of deference to the emperor. The following is part of the ruling made by the emperor denouncing Arius's teachings with fervor.

"In addition, if any writing composed by Arius should be found, it should be handed over to the flames, so that not only will the wickedness of his teaching be obliterated, but nothing will be left even to remind anyone of him. And I hereby make a public order, that if someone should be discovered to have hidden a writing composed by Arius, and not to have immediately brought it forward and destroyed it by fire, his penalty shall be death. As soon as he is discovered in this offense, he shall be submitted for capital punishment..."

— *Edict by Emperor Constantine against the Arians*[1]

However, as has been writ, "A mind changed against its will is of the same opinion still." As a result, the homousian party's victory at Nicaea was short-lived. Despite Arius's exile and the alleged finality of the Council's decrees, the controversy recommenced. When Bishop Alexander died in 327, Athanasius succeeded him.

Still committed to pacifying the conflict between Arians and Trinitarians, Constantine gradually became more lenient toward those whom the Council of Nicaea had exiled.][1] Although he never repudiated the council or its decrees, once Arius had reformulated his Christology to mute ideas found most objectionable by his critics, the emperor ultimately permitted Arius and many of his adherents to return to their homes. This time, in 335, Bishop Athanasius was exiled (though he was later recalled), and the Synod of Jerusalem the following year restored Arius to communion. The emperor directed Alexander of Constantinople to receive Arius, despite the bishop's objections. Bishop Alexander responded by earnestly praying that Arius might perish before this could happen.

With the likely help of poison, (ah Christianity) those prayers were answered. However, the death of Arius did not end the Arian controversy, which would not be settled for centuries in some parts of the Christian world. Constantine, who resisted baptism until on his deathbed, was baptized (probably not willingly) in 337 by the Arian bishop, Eusebius of Nicomedia

Also in 357, *The Seventh Arian Confession* (2nd Sirmium Confession) held, regarding the doctrines *homoousios* (of one substance) and *homoiousios* (of similar substance), that both were non-biblical; and that the Father is greater than the Son, a confession later dubbed the Blasphemy of Sirmia. But since many persons are disturbed by questions concerning what is called in Latin *substantia*, but in Greek *ousia*, that is, to make it understood more exactly, as to 'coessential', or what is called, 'like-in-essence', there ought to be no mention of any of these at all, nor exposition of them in the Church, for this reason and for this consideration, that in divine Scripture nothing is written about them, and that they are above men's knowledge and above men's understanding.

Well, how 'bout dem apples? Finally, an admission that YHVH is "Beyond our understanding!" And thence we come to the crux of it all, pun intended, of our overall problem with God: Our tendency, NO, NEED to anthropomorphize something so beyond our larval understanding. Just because scripture states we are created in His Image, even to providing our Creator with a gender specific pronoun, does not mean we can create YHVH in any atom of ours. The most accurate way to describe YHVH is as follows: "however, you can picture God, that ain't it." God be no bearded, white haired, be-robed grandfather in the clouds. What be He like? God be Love as illustrated by the life of that Son; a physical representation of The Father, not in physical form but in spiritual behavior as in "no one comes to the Father except through me" … not by magically professing a name but by living His essence in OUR EXISTANCE. As simple as that may sound, it still confounds many.

Our carnal inability to KNOW a Being composed (if that's even an acceptable concept) of Spirit goes even further. It deals with the mystery of time and space. Sort of like the Dr. Who concept of the *TARDIS* (Time and Relative Dimension in Space). "YHVH" as the Jews spelled God sans vowels, is not limited by such a physical construct. The point of God's declaration, "a year is as a thousand years and a thousand as but a year to Me is that YHVH doesn't dwell within time. Time is simply a means of measuring the decay of mortal organic life forms. Could it be that time itself will eventually be done away with? Rev. 22:5 Speaks of no more night: ***Ragnarök, the End of Days*** seems to be better food for thought than what the Arian/Athanasius Debate got so hung up on.

The Son was neither before, during, nor after because there was no passage of time; there just BE <u>being</u>. Neither does the headache inducing question of. what was before God?" have standing if there was no such thing as a before. The entire concept is beyond our ability to conceptualize. But, hey babe, ain't we got fun?

More came of the ensuing councils than just the eventual "let us not talk of it." While working towards the Canon of the first catholic (small c) Bible, the council also developed the initial Nicaean Creed. Finally, after making a big show of unity, the various members raced back to their individual ways pretty much acting as if nothing else had really been decided. Imagine what the process of grinding out the actual Bible sausage was going to be like. You guys include *James*, and we'll agree to the letters to *Timothy*...

Well, so much for the "every word of the Bible being the literal inerrant expression of God" proclamation... even allowing for errors in translation. But, but, wait! What about II Timothy 3:16-17 in which Paul declares all scripture to be God breathed and useful for teaching...etal? He could not have been referring to the Bible I use, since Paul's words of encouragement had yet to be published therein. As previously mentioned, what Paul was referring to were the Jewish prophetic books of the **Septuagint** from which Christ was prophesized. So, then, have we been leaning on a broken reed? Are we among the most miserable of men for hanging our souls on a false hope?

NO! Here to follow is why... the basis of what it is we DON'T GET!

For centuries Christianity has been playing telephone. The only reason it isn't worse is because, as Origen of Alexandria explained back in the 3rd

Century, that tortured tome pins the poetic moment for us to study and discuss. Just as in a poem the message can be interpreted one way or another for good or for bad. In the Bible we can both excuse and condemn slavery, war, and gender rights but to get it right requires prayer, study, common sense, and an ability to think outside the box.

First off, like the ancients, we still anthropomorphize this something that is far beyond our limited conception. The Arian controversy is a perfect example. The dispute hinged on the concept of Jesus begotten of the father. Well, how do you picture God? Is He an old bearded gray haired grandpa sitting up on his throne looking down through the clouds? That's what they call anthropomorphizing. One side felt that Jesus was less than God the father because he'd been begotten, therefore there had to be a time before he existed. God the father, on the other hand, was eternal with no beginning and no end. Now there's a hard nut for us physical clock watchers to crack. How could there not be a time before time? Gird up your loins. That dispute can be extinguished with a single reality check.

YHVH is so far beyond our ability to even imagine, God advises us, "Don't even try," in the commandment against creating ANY graven image of anything in Heaven or of God... Unless, that is, you follow the Catholic version of the 10 commandments which ignores and replaces that obvious second commandment by eliminating the offensive one and splitting the tenth into two. So, let's go back to the argument by Arius against the Word having not always existed.

(John 1:1 is a compelling argument against that). Since he was begotten as a son, He, therefore, could not be coequal with the father. Now I know this is all starting to sound rather ridiculous but follow along anyway. I really do have an endpoint which could be very encouraging to those of us who have been bamboozled by the slick haired snake oil salesmen.

So, then you ask, what is your point? My point is this: there is no such reality as before or after with God. Remember we already said that YHVH is eternal and been around for all time whatever time happens to be. So, is there actually such a thing as time in the first place or the last or those spaces in between or is time simply another creation for an unlimited Creator to use in the measurement of physical items that pass away... that rot, that deteriorate, or that have to be on time for work? So, let's twist a *Star Wars* quote from when Yoda states, "try... try? "There is no try; there is only do."

It's much the same with God. There is no after, there is no before, there is only **BE**! As God responded when Moses asked God who should I say sent me? "Say "I **Am**" has sent me." There is a world of hurt in that short little phrase. YHVH just is. And there's more to it than that. It's becoming apparent to me that time is merely a physical creation… that it is no more real than are we. God does not dwell within time. He doesn't exist, YHVH just is.

So, what do we have to represent God the father to us? We have the incarnate son; the physical avatar of our spiritual Creator born in our image and our physical limitations so that we can understand God by His behavior in the selfless way He lived His life -- by the way He represented the unknowable YHVH to us – a physical avatar of the spiritual realm. We were gifted with an example when He allowed Himself to be sacrificed for us; and, by doing so, He gained a first-hand understanding on what it is to be human. God willing, when I finish with this tome, the value of that self-effacing surrender will be all the more remarkable... to all of us. That would be the best physical representation of eternal Love.

Did Jesus really suffer on the cross because the Almighty unlimited creator of all that exists required it, or was it because we spiritually myopic humanoids needed to see blood sacrifice to believe our sins where covered? Go back and read how Jesus cried out, "Is this really necessary?" that night in Gethsemane. If so, that would make His sacrifice all the more meaningful.

But the corporate church derailed long ago and has never jumped back on the track. The efforts of Constantine and his popes, bishops, Cardinals, priests, and pastors to Follow LONG AGO decided to follow the money instead of the example of Jesus the Christ. They've been living off of us ever since, although on occasion some seem to get it…sort of…for a brief moment in time, although they still tend to wind up tripping over the same old stumbling blocks after shaking the dust off and shuffling on.

I hope to develop in the next chapters a doctrine of grace that truly few have come to understand. Those few I suspect that have, must keep it to themselves, since I haven't heard any hint of it. Have you? What about the eternity disguised in Genesis 1:2? There's someone that knows about that, because I have since read his work at Robert Clifton Robinson.com. While it was reassuring to discover philosophical support for my contentions, I just hope with divine help I can come to understand it more deeply, even as I struggle to explain it to everybody else.

But first, let's go over some other issues over which real thinkers like you tend to roll their eyes! Stay with me and we can begin to have some fun with this. At the very least you'll be able to stand your ground in a discussion regarding the geologic record, fossils, time, and the speed of light. However, I still see no evidence to support the <u>hypothesis</u> of evolution.

CHAPTER THREE

THE ROOT ISSUES

I was recently enjoying a beer while working on this particular manuscript when an older guy next to me said, pretty much out of the blue, "How can you look up into the immensity of the galaxy and say God created the heavens and the earth in six days?" Yeah, that really happened, believe it or not; his question, that is. I don't remember ever believing the point he was asking about. Besides, his statement was more of a challenge than a question, and I suppose he had been paying attention to my mad scribblings. It was a worthy observation, though, and one I was primed for and ready to discuss. But he wasn't yet through in his apparent attempt to stir up an argument.

He'd had a few before I'd even arrived, so I let this fish run out the line with other observations as I formatted my reply. He finished by heaping scorn on the story of Adam and Eve in the Garden of Eden. "What kind of a mighty all-knowing god would have allowed the devil to do that?" He was so smooth in his declaration I am certain this wasn't his first rodeo. Then he fixed me with a smirk as he awaited the expected stammering reply.

"Perhaps," I answered, "the entire creation myth is simply a metaphor with which to get across a lesson or make some sort of cosmic point." At this point he stared at me in complete surprise. I, in turn, was just as surprised at not being required to explain the poetic term. My fellow barfly was, apparently, an educated man.

After nodding his head in agreement, though, he went back to the roots of the issue. "How, then, do you explain the Bible narrative of creation? How could God have made everything in just six days? How could our universe be only six thousand years old when light from the stars in the sky has taken millennia just to reach and twinkle above us? Was that some sort of obscure allegory, too?"

"Perhaps," I began in an effort at softening the mood, "but, then again you are making the common error of mistranslating the first three verses. The literal translation of Genesis 1:1 simply begins with '***In the beginning, God***.'"

To this he nodded and said, "And the earth was without form and void."

"That is the common mistranslation," I said with a gentle smile. "But think about it. What the hell does that even mean? The narrative doesn't state that God began to form the earth out of nothing. It was already there, though not in any sort of life sustaining form. Was it an unformed collection of rocks, gasses, or a combination thereof?" He remained quiet awaiting my answer. Did God create it all that way, or was our world's state of being the result of some previous cataclysm?" I could tell I'd gotten his imagination fired up. Perhaps there was more than he'd imagined to the creation narrative.

"The answer hides within a <u>mistranslation</u> of these four words: ***was without form*** and ***void***. The first verb, **<u>was</u>**, derives from the original (*ha-ya-tah*) which is, elsewhere, used as a <u>transitive</u> verb better translated as ***became*** (2 Chron. 15:19, Isaiah 14:24 and 64:10, am 1:8). In Genesis 19:24 Lot's wife ***became*** a pillar of salt. The other participants in this translation, *without form* and *void*, derive from the root words *tohu wa bohu*. Elsewhere in scripture (Isaiah 34:11 and Jer. 4:23) they are used to describe a state of being after a land has been ravaged by war. The proper, and more representative description would be the following: but *the earth had been ravaged and turned into a wasteland*. After which God brooded over what was left before beginning a restructuring of this earth complete with a fossil record of the previous world."

To his blank stare, I struggled to keep from shouting out in frustration, "Don't you get it? All those evolutionist arguments rot away with a realistic interpretation of those first verses of the Genesis record. Scripture and science are in concord."

Obviously, this was not something he had expected to hear. He began to nod despite the doubt still showing in his eyes. Without getting in too deep, I simply wanted to deal with the huge religious gorilla in the dialog. I took a deep breath and went on. "In accordance with this narrative, the heavens and the earth could be of any age that science might deduce from the fossil record, the speed of light, or radiometric dating. That may have had to do with how long it took to create the oil, gas, coal, and other minerals so necessary to modern humanity."

He finally laughed. "I have never in my life heard anything so…"

'Ridiculous," I offered?

"No, outlandish would be more my thinking, though… I doubt if that sort of talk would make you too popular with hard core Bible thumpers. Where do you attend?" He laughed again. "It might be entertaining to watch you stir things up."

My response of 'I've been unaffiliated for more than the past decade," didn't require too much further explanation of what I'd already learned the hard way. "No priest or pastor willingly suffers a heretic like me stirring up the sacred balance of their congregation with uncomfortable questions. Besides, who am I to disturb the comfort of someone's blind faith. Tis fellow spiritual vagabonds like you to whom I am attracted."

However," he offered, "I have heard it proposed by a few that God, being all powerful, could have created the earth and universe in situ."

"With a faked history?" I asked incredulously. "Wouldn't that have made God into a liar?" As usual, that effectively ended such a self-deceiving speculation.

From there he and I went on to the Bible and how much of it was true and how much might be allegorical with him pointing out it hadn't been compiled until the 4th century A.D. I, then, showed him the first paragraph of what I had previously written which stated the same fact. After laughing together over memories of playing the word share game of telephone, we finally parted company with him struggling to digest data he had never heard before. I left for home thankful for having been gifted with inspiration on how to begin this chapter of my treatise.

From what I can determine, not much was truly accomplished at this 1st *Council of Nicaea* other than mandating a uniform date during which to observe **Easter** and booting 21 books from the proposed Bible canon. Of course, Jesus is still being forced to experience the three days and nights between Good Friday and Easter Sunday morning twice a year, since the *Roman Catholic Church* and *Eastern Orthodox Churches* were not able to agree on whether to figure the actual dates from out of the Gregorian or Julian calendars. Between that and the reality that the *Arian Controversy* continued to be a waste of time and effort, one wonders just what was accomplished?

With the support of Bishop Eusebius, who argued against homousian thought, Arius was reinstated in 335 AD. In the same year Constantine deposed Arius's rival, Bishop Athanasius, further muddying the waters of the baptismal pool. Other than penning the

Nicene Creed, the attendees couldn't seem to manage unanimous consent on much of anything else... except maybe, "don't piss off the emperor!" So much for inspiration. With that in mind, the struggle upon which words were to be considered as God's and which were not worthy for inclusion in the Bible should prove to be most thought provoking.

The first issue to deal with was, since there was no Bible to wave back during "Biblical Times," just how was Jesus preached to the faithful? I remember my pastor waving his Bible, during one of my last appearances in a formal church gathering, and proclaiming "...however, we have God's word to show us the truth." The truth of his point aside, the church back then didn't have a book like that to wave. So, what did they have. How did the churches of the era manage without it?

There were two separate sources from which to preach the Gospel (good news): The Jewish prophecies, compiled into the Greek language Old Testament collection known as the *Septuagint*, and the letters of Paul written to deal with the issues of various elders and their churches. These epistles grew in stature as they were shared about. By the time they achieved the official rank of scripture, at the A.D. 393 *Council of*

Hippo, they had long since been considered as such by the congregations.

The writings of the Apostle Paul account for up to 14 of the 27 New Testament "books." Though only 7 of them are 100% certain. Eleven epistles were written before the first of the Gospels, of Luke, was penned. Four more were written before the Gospels of Mark and Matthew. The Gospel and three epistles of St. John were the final books written, coming even after the Apocalypse was revealed by John at the end of his life.

So, since the little flock was doing so well as it was, why expend the efforts required to canonize these writings into a holy collection? Why indeed: The key is contained in the term, canonized (approved) scriptures. The old adage of "follow the money" also holds true here, as well. The 27 were not the only "scriptures" floating about nor were they all of one accord. The Sword of Constantine was still in control. Rome required the all-conquering *First Horseman of the Apocalypse* in order to maintain the required narrative.

The process of elimination first begun at the 1st Council of Nicaea forged on, first with the Apocrypha, and then through the next two centuries as various writings were excluded, reinstated, and separated into competing biblical variations. Were all of these the inerrant inspired words of God? With that kind of a deity in charge of sacred writ, is it any wonder Satan was able to sneak into the Garden of Eden to *pave over Paradise and put in a parking lot?* Nor is it any surprise logical thinkers, on both sides of the issue, cast doubts upon the arguments of church apologists.

So, here's the deal from my perspective: This was a political rather than a religious move by Emperor Constantine. The base issue for him had to do with maintaining *Pax Romana* throughout the empire. Disputes amongst his priesthood were not to be permitted. Hence, anything stirring up even the potential for dissension, was unacceptable. And, if a particular narrative was to be ordained, that which best proclaimed the divine nature of Jesus was preferred... at spearpoint if necessary.

All those scriptural accounts rolling around the churches like shipboard loose cannons on storm tossed seas were to be... shall we say, restrained. So, God's broth was to be reduced and thickened like so much gravy. Anything illustrating the humanity of Jesus was tossed. "There were," it was argued, "only so many placeholders available if the new handbook was to be kept manageable. Is it any wonder Holy Scripture leans so heavily upon the concept of "obey those who have the rule over you," and "slaves, obey your masters as you would the Lord?" Since that fairly screams "State Religion," what went wrong?

As far as those insisting ALL scripture is true and inerrant, consider the stir csused by Galileo Galilei. When he set out to prove the heliocentric nature of earth orbit he was accused of denying Holy Scriptures like I Chron. 16:30, Eccl. 1:5, Ps.104 :19-21, and others mentioned in Chapter 24 "that the earth moveth not," or that "The Sun goeth down and travels around to where it riseth up again." Obviously, the scriptures are allegorical rather than literal. But there are still folks about…

It's surprising that, despite the nefarious efforts of the Inquisition and their red robed masters, we still ended up with far more than THE one "acceptable version" of the Bible. I don't mean the obvious variations like the King James, Living Bible, New international Version, and many other such variations. Depending on if you're an Orthodox Christian, Catholic, or Protestant, there are basic differences in the Bible's makeup. Throughout history the Bible canon has been changed, with some books being added and others removed. In addition, some versions are more 'academic' with additional information, and others embracing different manuscripts not found in mainstream versions.

The 'official' Bible has been modified over the last 1700 years. As already mentioned, the initial attempt to create a standardized version was in 325 A.D., when Emperor Constantine gave an order for 50 copies to be compiled. However, it wasn't until 367 A.D., when Bishop Athanasius of Alexandria listed the books that should be included in the New Testament, that the official canon of the Bible was developed. Excluded were such interesting manuscripts as the Revelation of Peter, the Epistles of Barnabas and Clement, the *Infancy Gospel* (dealing with the youth of Jesus), the *Gospel of Mary (rejected due to sexism) along with the Acts of Paul and Thecla*, as well as a few others that might have added an understanding of "Jesus the man" but didn't follow the chosen narrative of Constantine's church.

Other edits came during the Protestant Reformation when significant changes were made to Christianity itself in the face of increasingly questionable actions by the ruling Robes. Finally, a Catholic monk, Martin Luther, rebelled against the indulgences and other sinful practices of his own Roman Catholic Church, and the Protestant Movement was born. The Church of England appeared from the Protestant movement, along with the 16th century King James version of the Bible. At this time, the invention of the printing press made the ability to print and distribute a standard version of the Bible far easier. At long last, the general public had private access, though still reliant upon educated eyes to read them.

Today, except for those totally destroyed back in the 4th Century, we can all have reference to these forbidden writings. The authorities will no longer come looking for us, at least not yet. The only penalty we risk is "cancellation." There are, however, enough of us old folks who no longer care about such a superficial threat. Heck, it might even be worthwhile to go out in a blaze of glory. With that in mind, as I continue trying to make sense of what God be doing, read on and help me get this derailed soul train back on the tracks.

CHAPTER FOUR

PROCLAIMING THE GOOD NEWS

Way back some 300 years before the Bible became available, the Gospel message of Jesus was ready to be shared. The individual God chose to carry this message to the world says a lot of what we don't get about God. **Saul of Tarsus**, often referred to as Saul the Destroyer, was the antithesis of who we might imagine for the role.

Saul of Tarsus was born in approximately AD 5 in the city of Tarsus in Cilicia (in modern-day Turkey). He was born to Jewish parents who possessed Roman citizenship, a coveted privilege that their son would also possess. This would work very strongly to his advantage during his travels throughout the empire.

After being moved to Jerusalem, sometime between AD 15—20, Saul began his studies of the Hebrew Scriptures in the city of Jerusalem. It was under **Gamaliel** that Saul would begin an in-depth study of the Law with the highly respected rabbi. In his second letter to the church in Corinth, Paul described himself as a Hebrew, an Israelite, and a descendant of Abraham. In his letter to the Philippian church Paul's post-conversion correspondence to various churches reveals even more about his background. Paul says he was a Pharisee of the tribe of Benjamin.

It is written that Saul was present, serving as a cloak check, for the trial of Stephen—a trial that resulted in Stephen becoming the first Christian martyr. The historian Luke tells us that Stephen's executioners laid their garments at the feet of Saul, who was in full approval of the mob's murderous actions. Saul later ravaged the church, entering the homes of believers and committing them to prison. Saul's anti-Christian zeal motivated him not only to arrest and imprison male Christians (the "ringleaders") but to lock up female believers as well.

Saul's education, his background as a Pharisee, his Roman citizenship, and his unflagging zeal all contributed to his success as a missionary once those credentials and traits had been subjugated to the lordship of Christ. Most effective, however, was the credibility his original focus emphasized his conversion to his former targets. God could not have chosen a better foil with which to proclaim His Gospel to the non-Jewish Roman world. His singular weakness, however, would further emphasize that thing we fail to fully grasp: the power of Grace. While his letters to the various churches were described as powerful, his personal appearance was described as rather less impressive. So, acting as Saul, his overemphasis on persecuting the new sect may have been overcompensation for his overly pedantic, 'thorn in the flesh,' even effeminate, appearance.

While on his way to Damascus to arrest and extradite Christians back to Jerusalem, Saul was confronted by the One whom he was persecuting. What followed was one of the most dramatic conversions in church history. Saul of Tarsus became the apostle Paul, an ardent missionary to an unbelieving world and the ultimate example of faithful service in the face of fierce persecution.

How accurate the Biblical account may be, something extraordinary certainly occurred. So, let's play it straight as we imagine Saul leading his cohort of soldiers into the future. As he headed towards the impending confrontation, Saul considered the possible implications. He was nearing the age of 30, when leadership positions would begin opening up for him. After Stephen's death, Saul had launched a campaign against the new Jewish heresy. He was not yet the one in charge, but Paul, threatening with every breath and eager to destroy every follower of the Jesus heresy, went to the High Priest in Jerusalem. He requested a letter addressed to synagogues in Damascus, requiring their cooperation in the persecution of any believers he found there, both men and women, so that he could bring them in chains to Jerusalem.

As he approached Damascus on this mission, the young rabbinical candidate struggled with whether his campaign of persecution had been designed to make a name for himself. Once so established, he could assume a leadership role when one became available. His focus was so strong that he often wondered, *"But am I guilty of covetousness?"*

If Saul coveted power, his persecution of heretics would have been an excellent means to attain the rank of a respected member of Jewish society. This is what makes his conversion into Paul, the apostle of Jesus, so remarkably effective. To suddenly jump from one extreme to the other and lose all the advantages he had struggled to attain proves the reality of his conversion experience. He had but to attain the age of thirty and his future would have been assured. Until, that is, he was confronted by the newly risen Messiah.

Suddenly a brilliant light from heaven flooded him![4] Saul fell to the ground and heard a voice saying to him, "Saul! Saul! Why are you persecuting me?"

"Who is speaking?" Paul asked.

"I am Jesus, the one you are persecuting! Now get up and go into the city and await my further instructions."

The men with Paul stood speechless with surprise, for they heard the sound of someone's voice but saw no one! As Saul struggled to pick himself up off the ground, he realized he was blind. He had to be led into Damascus and was there three days, blind, going without food and water all that time.

Now there was in Damascus a believer named Ananias. The Lord spoke to him in a vision, calling, "Ananias!"

"Yes, Lord!" he replied.

And the Lord said, "Go over to Straight Street and find the house of a man named Judas and ask there for Saul of Tarsus. He is praying to me right now, for I have shown him a vision of a man named Ananias coming in and laying his hands on him so that he can see again!"

"But Lord," Ananias cried out in horror, "I have heard about the terrible things this man has done to the believers in Jerusalem![14] And we hear that he has arrest warrants with him from the chief priests, authorizing him to arrest every believer in Damascus!"

But the Lord said, "Just do it! Paul is my chosen instrument to take my message to the nations and before kings, as well as to the people of Israel. Don't worry, I will show him how much he must suffer for me."

So, Ananias sucked it up, found Paul, laid his hands on him and said, "Brother Paul, the Lord, who appeared to you on the road, has sent me that you may be filled with the Holy Spirit and get your sight back."

[18]Instantly (it was as though scales fell from his eyes) Paul could see and was immediately baptized. Then he ate and was strengthened. Saul hung out with the believers in Damascus for a few days before heading over to the synagogue to tell everyone there the Good News about Jesus—that he is indeed the Son of God!

"Whoa dude!" All who heard him were amazed. "Isn't this the same man who persecuted Jesus' followers so bitterly in Jerusalem?" they asked. "And didn't he come here to arrest and drag them in chains to the chief priests?"

As Saul became more and more fervent in his preaching, the Damascus Jews couldn't withstand his proofs that Jesus was indeed the Christ. It wasn't long, nor surprising that the Jewish leaders determined to silence him. But, having been warned they were watching the gates of the city day and night prepared to murder him, during the night some of his converts let him down in a basket through an opening in the city wall, and he escaped!

Upon returning to Jerusalem, he sought to meet with the believers, but they were all afraid of him. They thought he was faking![27] Then Barnabas brought him to the apostles and told them how Paul had seen the Lord on the way to Damascus, what the Lord had said to him, and all about his powerful preaching in the name of Jesus.[28] Then they accepted him, and after that he was constantly with the believers and preached boldly in the name of the Lord. But then some Greek-speaking Jews with whom he had argued plotted to murder him. However, when the other believers heard about his danger, they took him to Caesarea and then sent him to his home in Tarsus.

Meanwhile, with their chief persecutor having switched benches, the church had peace throughout Judea, Galilee, and Samaria, and grew in strength and numbers. The believers learned how to **behave in respect** of the Lord and in the comfort of the Holy Spirit. And all this occurred long before the Bible came to be. Then the eternal God motivated his chosen tool to open his mouth one time too many and the Roman campaign began.

CHAPTER FIVE

WHEN IN ROME

In keeping with the "what we don't get about God" theme, the commonly understood aspects of Paul's evangelical efforts throughout the Jewish communities of Asia Minor will be skipped over in deference to his effect upon Roman culture. His stature as a Roman citizen protected him from the local religious leaders, but ensured he would end up before Caesar sooner or later. That was obviously God's intent.

After returning from his third evangelical journey Paul went to Jerusalem for the last time to meet with 'James and the *elders to distribute the contributions he had collected for the destitute suffering there. By this time Paul had, possibly, forgotten how the Jews felt about him mingling with "unclean" Gentiles. Chafing under Roman rule, they were ready to openly rebel. Wasn't the Messiah supposed to drive out these foreigners and restore the Kingdom of Israel? It was bad enough that Paul mixed with them while away on business, but when he brought a gang of them back to the Holy City... that was too much for them to accept.

The religious leaders thought Saul. as Paul, had turned traitor and was teaching false doctrine to the foreign Jews to appease the hated Romans. Now, here he was back, intent on violating the Law of Moses. After he was accused of taking a Gentile into the temple the excrement hit the fan.

Those Jews now saw Paul in the Temple. A crowd quickly gathered. There were arguments and a fight. Paul was in great danger, but Roman soldiers saved him from the mob. Although Paul knew he had many enemies in Jerusalem, he had failed to consider how strongly his enemies opposed him.

After the soldiers rescued Paul he was allowed to speak to the crowd, They listened to him in silence when he talked about the living Lord Jesus, but as soon as he mentioned the gentiles, the mob began to shout him down. The soldiers sought to calm things down by laying hold of Paul, but when he advised them, he was a Roman citizen, they backed off. They could not strike a Roman citizen.

The next day the Roman commander brought Paul to the Sanhedrin. Some of the Sanhedrin were Sadducees. Sadducees did not believe in life after death. But some of them were Pharisees, who did believe in life after death. Paul, who was well aware of this, made full use of his trump card to stir things up. So, as soon as he could, he spoke about resurrection from death, and the two factions began a fierce argument. To his amusement, the Romans had to rescue Paul again.

After this, when a plot to kill Paul was revealed, he notified the Romans. who sent Paul with soldiers to Felix, the governor of Caesarea. The Roman commander included a letter explaining he wasn't able to make any accusation of Paul, Felix arranged for the high priest and his friends to go to Caesarea where they had sufficient authority to do so. After thanking Felix for the 'period of peace' during his rule, the High Priest accused Paul of disturbing that peace adding Paul had spoiled the Temple. However, lacking any sort of proof, Felix sent them packing.

Afterwards Felix and his companion Drusilla talked with Paul. Paul spoke to them about goodness. He said that men must control their behavior. He spoke about the judgement that will come. This worried Felix, and he talked with Paul many times. Still seeking to please the Jews, though, Felix left Paul in prison until Festus took over as the next governor after which it was deja' Vieux all over again.

Of course, when Festus brought Paul to court again the Jews, who had authority, were there seeking to extradite him. Once again, with no verdict taken, the suggestion was made for the troublemaker to be returned to court in Jerusalem. Paul, aware of the dangers of such a move, appealed for his right as a Roman citizen to be judged by Caesar. Festus agreed. Soldiers would take Paul to Rome.

Before Paul left, King Agrippa came to visit Festus. Not knowing what to say about Paul in a letter to Rome, he asked Agrippa to examine him. Paul went through the entire spiel about his early life, how he became a Christian, his travels, and about his work. Paul reminded Agrippa about the prophecies about the Messiah. Jesus proved that these prophecies were true.

King Agrippa and Festus agreed on one thing. If Paul had not appealed to Caesar, they might have freed him. (But, with a price on his head, if Paul had not done so, he would probably have been assassinated.

As it turned out, Paul was in prison at Caesarea for two years or more. Luke was one of his companions.

After he was transported under guard via ship to Rome (a journey that included a shipwreck on Malta) and spent a couple more years under house arrest in Rome. End of story? No. That's where the book of Acts ends, but it is not the end of the story. Here is a brief recounting of events in Paul's *fourth* missionary journey in their likely sequence.

Following his house arrest in Rome, Paul was released by Nero. The early church historian Eusebius writing about AD 325 supported this with his claim that Paul's martyrdom wasn't during this period.

Clement, writing around AD 95 *in Rome*, writes that Paul "after he had preached in the East and in the West, he won genuine glory, having taught righteousness to the whole world and reached the"- farthest limits of the West" which *usually* meant Spain. After his return, Paul sailed to the island of Crete where he engaged in ministry alongside Titus. Afterwards he left Titus to appoint elders in the cities that held believing communities. Paul then, traveled to Ephesus to meet with Timothy.

During Paul's remaining time he likely visited the various churches in Macedonia until Nero had him arrested.

After Paul's arrest, he was taken to Rome and imprisoned, not in a house as during his former internment, but in the notorious **Mamertine Prison** around the time that Nero started to unleash a horrific wave of persecution against Christians in Rome. During his time in prison, Paul resumed penning the various epistles that make up much of the New Testament. Paul was aided by the physician Luke, who sought to attend to his needs (2 Tim 4:18).

Paul is believed to have been beheaded—rather than thrown to the wild beasts or killed in some other inhumane way—because he was a Roman citizen. Prior to all this there occurred an event that radically altered the attitude of the church.

CHAPTER SIX

DARKNESS DESCENDS

Then, in rode Jesus on his chopper, GRACE, ruffling robes & stirring up dust on the Temple Mount.

A Quick Review, because
some explanations require that a story be told:

Long ago God, beyond the reach of common man, was viewed as some sort of vengeful spirit. The people, whose main interest was in bringing home the bacon without becoming it, addressed their deities through ceremony and ritual. A priestly order rose itself up to take charge of such things, sort of a marriage of Jerry Falwell and Hillary Clinton, represent the people to God, and conversely, God to the people. In those days, church and state were synonymous. Sort of like, the televangelist "requesting" your donation about the same time a swat team would show up at the door to "collect" it.

This was a rather neat little arrangement. Nobody needed to think about much other than tending to their physical needs, a daunting enough task in that age, and the priests stood to make a comfortable living from their cut of the payoff they extorted from the common folk. Into this neat little arrangement rode Jesus, as it were rapping the pipes of his Harley and stirring up dust on the temple mount.

Nobody really knew what this stranger wanted, not even the scruffy gang of disciples he'd recruited. The downtrodden thought he had come to lead a rebellion overthrowing the Roman occupational forces and restore the majesty Israel had previously known. The Priests, who could read his credentials quite well, thank you, feared he would get them all kicked out of their cushy gig. At the very least, he was giving instructions that they should humble themselves to the point of washing feet. YUCK! At worst, he was going to get them offed by their Roman overlords.

Even the Disciples argued over who would get the best positions when he took over. But all this dude did was take his ride from town to town talking in strange parables, hanging around with people from the other side of the chariot tracks, and teaching some strange new concept: "Love your enemies?" Another Commie liberal upsetting "prophet" margins.

Finally, Judas had had enough. See, this Judas guy was the treasurer; he carried the bag for www.Jesus.org and stood to make a tidy little bundle on the side if this Jesus guy would ever get off the stick and start the ball rolling. With the miracles this character could pull off, why the sky would be the limit -- or not. But, how to get him to start doing the Sylvester Stallone bit on the bad guys?

Well, Judas comes up with an idea to provoke this miracle worker into action. He decides to pretend to turn traitor, for a nice little bribe of course. However, things don't go his way when the authorities bust Jesus and give him such a beating (all in the name of God of course) that the original love child is left looking like raw hamburger. The "Robes and Suits" get together and hold "one of those trials." But the Roman Governor, of all people, doesn't buy any of it and tries to give him an out. The priests have a full force hissy fit, and get their way; 'cause, as usual, the only thing government is really interested in is satisfying the big contributors.

Before anyone knows what's happening, the priests have organized their mob beginning the Easter Parade tradition. The guest of honor is dragged up to the killing hill where they nail him up to a cross or a pole or whatever to die the famous slow death. Some soldier, motivated by the priests who require him to be dead and buried before the beginning of their weeklong Passover Party, sticks him with a sword, and Jesus bleeds out ending his misery – see, there is mercy in the world.

Well, this was not at all what Judas was expecting. With Jesus dead and all the disciples scattered (I told you these guys didn't get the picture), Judas sees his hopes for riches severely downsized. If this had been Wall Street, he'd of jumped out a window. Instead he settled for hanging himself after tossing the blood money in a potter's field which leads to some saying I don't remember or care about. Maybe that's how they came up with the name of the crooked old banker in that iconic Jimmy Stewart Christmas movie -- whatever.

The point of all this is what?... Oh, yeah, that nobody had a clue what Jesus was about (also a continuing tradition). Three days and nights later (try fitting that into the Good Friday sunset to Easter Sunday tradition) he came to himself and left the tomb to show himself and get the show on the road. As Paul would later point out, "These things weren't done in a corner." There were lots of witnesses – and, no, I don't mean those guys who show up knocking at our doors.

As for the "The Passover Plot" theory: well, if it had been just a plot to fake it all, Jesus' buddies wouldn't have been so quick to run off and hide. Hey, his main guy Peter, when asked what he would do now, said, "I'm going fishing" (And, even more so, later they certainly would not have been so keen about dying for a lie).

So, Peter shoved off in his boat wondering how he could have been so wrong about everything – apparently including where the fish are. Then, Jesus shows up on the shore and yells out to Peter and his fishing buddies. "Hey guys, how's the fishing?"

Peter, who doesn't recognize Jesus, He must have hidden the Harley and disguised Himself, yells back, "It sucks!" (Hey, this is how fishermen have talked ever since)

So, Jesus, always one to make a scene, yells back, "You're fishing on the wrong side of the boat; throw the nets on the other side."

Yeah right, can you just imagine what Peter thought? "What kind of fool is this, anyway? What does he think; the fish are sticking their tongues out at us from behind?" But he goes and does it cause fishermen will try ANYTHING to catch fish, and behold, there are so many fish in the net, they can't pull it in.

Peter, like totally freaks out, man. He goes, "Jeez, it's the Lord, guys; and they row the boat ashore [I don't know if some guy named Michael was there or not). Then they have a big fish fry (must-of been Friday night, yahey?). Even Jesus has some fish which is good to know because he's like dead and resurrected and he can still turn down the volume on his Glory, kick back, and break some bread, man. Kuool!

Yeah, I think that is really great to know, what with most Jesus freaks thinking dead people have nothing better to look forward to than sitting around on glorified soap suds and staring at bright lights. Around here, you can do something like that with peyote. The sun will blind you (it's not even close to as bright as God) and the best you can do is act like an Indian holy man and live off alms, but whatever.

Anyway, Jesus is resurrected, showing there's something more to life than blood, sweat, and tears. BUT he fails to hang around to defeat the Romans like everyone expected. Unfortunately, the disciples, who were left with his Harley, can't figure out how to ride it. Every time they try, they get tossed into jail for disturbing the Pax. As previously explained, this was no everyday Harley; it was a custom chopper.

It was, like, all chrome with super extended forks. The front wheel stuck out so far, Jesus knew what was coming days before he'd get there. Most people can't deal with that kind of foresight, so it made the chopper really hard to handle. The saddle was, like, totally low slung and there were no shock absorbers; Jesus wanted to be able to feel close and in touch with the earth as he passed over it. That kind of ride would kick the… uh, the daylights out of anybody else.

The totally weird thing was, there were no handlebars to steer with. Jesus had enough trust to leave all control up to a higher authority. To finish off the picture, the chopper had straight pipes – big old quads. There would be no quiet cruising around for Jesus. You'd know when he was coming, and you would damn well know when he was around. Long after he had left, the message of his passing lingered in the air.

This was one mean motorcycle, Daddy' Oh. So, God decided to look around for someone who'd know how to handle His special ride.

Now, one thing to keep in mind when you're dealing with God, is that He never does ANYTHING the way you think He should. So, in this case, God settles on a really bad dude referred to as Saul the Destroyer. From a distance he sounded like a pro wrestler and was about as bad as one. His job is to ride around on his Honda Gold Wing, chasing down followers of the new sect and beating the be-Jesus out of them (Hey, that IS what he did; I'm just relating the story, dude).

Well, Saul is tooling along with his strike force, when God knocks him right off his ride. What I think happened here, is that God suspended time and space for everything but Saul, who kept on going when the bike and his buddies froze in time. Saul hits the ground like there's no tomorrow and when finally comes to, he's like that Indian mystic who sat eating peyote and staring at the sun; stone cold blind, but he's got a head full of reformatted data. I guess if you're going to have to ride a chopper with no handlebars, being able to see would be somewhat over rated, as well. God changes his name to Paul, tells him to go see some of his people who will restore his sight (Sort of like a sign or something).

Well, when he gets to the house where the Harley has been hidden (remember, these people are hiding in fear of the very bad dude who shows up at the door), everybody freaks. Even though Paul (Saul) insists he's seen the light (literally) and been sent there by God. The dude at the door turns white, tells Paul to hang loose while he ducks back in to talk to God like God doesn't realize Paul's real identity. Jesus was like that, too, hanging with and drinking wine the wrong kind of people.

God tells him to get with it, and, after giving Paul the Word, he pulls out the Harley and gives it a look over. Paul is blown away! He's the perfect dude to handle Jesus' Ride. Everywhere he goes, the sound of his pipes stir the dust of emotions. He even annoys the very people who think they understand what Jesus was about (I know, I know – that hasn't change much, either). Eventually he's arrested and shipped off to Rom.

While in preparation for his potential final position of lion trainer, Paul sends out recordings of his chopper's pipes dealing with how we should behave if we want to be real *Jesus People*. There's just one thing wrong with this; only the people in charge know how to read and Gutenberg hasn't been born yet. So, once again, the job of "interpreting" God's will for the many is taken over by the few. Once Paul and his buddies die, Tribulation and Famine of the Word set in. Despite history, these days it's only a surprise to folks who believe it has yet to occur.

Without Peter and Paul around (and Mary died long before) to keep things under control, arguments raged back and forth. Nobody could agree on anything -- even whether Jesus was divine (*God in the flesh*) or just a man *begotten of God* for this purpose. They couldn't agree whether to meet on Saturday as before or Sunday in honor of the resurrection or, for that matter, on which Sunday to celebrate Easter. Most of this was really about who would be in control -- remember Judas?

The Roman Emperor at the conclusion of the Great Persecution was Constantine. He didn't care diddle about anything but restoring order to the empire, so he took an interest in the new and growing sect of Christianity. If he could get Rome to embrace this new faith (which taught obedience to the government) he could stabilize a tottering kingdom (er -- empire). He ordered the quibbling bishops to get together and settle their differences. When they couldn't agree, he told them what to decide. They all avowed, "Sure, boss," then went their way still disagreeing in private.

The Faith was now a possession of the state; I'm sure you realize this was not a good thing.

A church, with sufficient mass to create its own field of gravity, was formed wherein all things were to be decided in a corporate manner. If you disagreed, you got downsized headfirst or you became the star attraction at a community cook out. Since they held all the cards, their word was law. Nobody could adequately dispute their authority. There was still no Bible available and few manuscripts to be had. "Joe the Plumber" couldn't read, and the church taught education (like cleanliness) was of the devil. Fear and ignorance held the field. It was like a Hell's Angels Convention in a church, except these guys were really "power ties" disguised under linen robes. Since nobody could ride the Chopper, it was set on top of a monument as a symbol of the crucifixion, where the crux holds court to this very day.

With apologies for my free-wheeling run on the *Chopper of Grace*, it was a useful ride through the flow of history. From the end of the *1st century Apostolic Era to the Edic of Milan* in 313 the persecuted followers of ***The Way*** met secretly in private house churches without any overall organization. Hence variety was, to say the least, the "order" of observance. As has been pointed out, various sects were often in violent dispute over the divine nature of Jesus. After the Tribulation instituted by Emperor Nero, the influence of Constantine must have seemed to be a godsend.

Nero Claudius Augustus Germanicus had been everything bad we can imagine in a Roman Caesar; tyrannical, self-indulgent, and debauched. His mother, Agrippina the Younger, doing a classic impression of Cruella De 'Ville, had poisoned his adoptive father, Emperor Claudius, so their son could succeed him to the throne. Nero, tiring of his mother's control issues, eventually had her murdered as well as knocking off certain others of his family… and this is the guy from whom Paul had hoped to get a fair trial? Phat chance, that, in more ways than one.

After he was accused of igniting the great fire of 64 A.D., Nero had shifted blame to adherents of the annoying new Jewish sect referred to as Christians thereby igniting the Great Persecution which resulted in the martyrdom of scores of Christians including the apostles Peter and Paul. For the next two centuries Christianity descended into a darkness which varied depending on the whim of the emperor of the moment. Do not simply pass lightly over that fact. Go back and reread it while picturing what horrors these saints suffered for their faith with whole families being torn apart in the Colosseum by beasts, burnt alive, crucified along the sides of the Apian Way, and hiding out of sight in the depths of the Roman Catacombs!!! If that doesn't qualify the vocalization of the word, Tribulation, I shudder to imagine what more would be required. Is it any wonder that the church which emerged from hiding at the beginning of the 4th Century bore little resemblance to the original "little flock of Jesus." And that was just the beginning of what would develop.

This was no longer the same flock Paul had envisioned. It was more in line with that of James and the Jerusalem legalists with a growing emphasis on a list of "does and don'ts." And, as might have been expected with an assembly fractured into many pieces, like the dispute between Arius and Athanasius, by the necessity of laying low for multiple decades, arguments over issues of doctrine and procedure, even leading to bloodshed, began to break out. In his best attempt at reigning in "this mob of cats," the new emperor hosted the ***Council of Nicaea***. The ultimate result of this would produce the eventual ceremonial leavening complete with Priests, Bishops, Cardinals, Popes, sacraments, graven idols, and GUILT.

The Apostle Paul had strongly cautioned against the very legalism this corporate church was now basing its doctrine upon. In his first letter to Timothy, Paul had condemned "certain men who forbade marriage and advocated abstaining from certain foods were promoting doctrines of demons." That was then, 300 years before, and this was now. And the Bible still had not yet been written, let alone read by a mostly illiterate population content to freely breathe the fresh air. Issues of doctrine were now in the hands of those focused on gaining and maintaining control.

After Constantine the Great had defeated his rival Maxentius at the *Battle of the Milvian Bridge* in 312 A.D, the new Emperor Invictus had related his vision of a flaming cross descending from the heavens with the command "by this shall you conquer." In 313 A.D, his *Edict of Milan* officially put an end to the Great Persecution, permitting the observance of all religions. Behind the scenes, Constantine began his process of establishing Christianity as state religion of the proposed Holy Roman Empire. It was Constantine who ordered that the cross should replace the iconic fish image. On March 7, 321, in honor of *dies Sol Invictus*, Constantine decreed Sunday would be the official day of rest throughout the empire. The church went along with the change due to the erroneous belief that Jesus had been raised on a Sunday.

So, the expected question is raised: if God was truly in control of circumstances, why would he allow His word to be mis-used. Indeed, that is a fair question and one worth including with the question "why does He allow evil in the first place?" My best guess, in answer to this most common of questions, relates back to that bite into the fruit from **The Tree of the Knowledge of Good and Evil**. How better to teach the lesson of why not to touch the hot stove and most effectively develop r9ighteous free will?

CHAPTER SEVEN

THE POETIC MOMENT

In explanation, the ***poetic moment*** (heuristic device) relates to the real and surreal with layers of reception and perception (Implicative lacunae) leading the obvious to transcend into deeper contemplation. In other words, a poet visualizes a subject and paints it with words. A reader, then, interprets those words back into imagery which may or may not reflect the intent of the poet. Any "poetic" attempt to <u>instruct</u> readers what to see is, at best, simply rhymed essay. Tis best to keep that in mind when studying the divinely inspired meaning of scripture.

While the chief public reference of Christianity is the Bible, no other collection of writings has generated more disagreement. One side considers every jot and tittle as the very inerrant words of God; others, even including former Pope Leo X, dismiss portions of it as fables. As has been shown, the first four centuries of the "church" managed without it. So, a natural question arises; should it be discounted altogether or studied as the inspired words of sincere men attempting to understand God?

Obviously, the solution to this conundrum is fraught with considerable hazard and controversy. The correct path to follow is contained within the word, considerable – consider. We need to deeply consider the "poetic moment" painted by the words. In Paul's 2nd letter to Timothy, the very scripture used by literalists to assert the divine nature of the Bible is used to emphasize the importance of carefully interpreting the word of truth as in a poem's imagery. Look to the explanation given by Jesus as to why he taught using parables. (Matt. 13:10-12)

Keep in mind the scriptures Paul was referencing were not from the Holy Bible but Jewish prophecies from the 3rd Century BCE Septuagint. However, since the early followers of Jesus had many of the original apostolic letters as well as those Old Testament scriptures, that admonition to "rightly interpret" holds true today.

One of Paul's epistles, that to the Colossian Congregation, holds admonitions on avoiding the errors into which the Roman Church fell.

(Col 3:16) Therefore, let no one pass judgment on you in questions of food and drink, or with regard to a festival or a new moon or a Sabbath. 17 These are a shadow of the things to come, but the substance belongs to Christ.[18] Let no one disqualify you, insisting on asceticism and worship of angels, going on in detail about visions,[d] puffed up without reason by his sensuous mind,[19] and not holding fast to the Head, from whom the whole body, nourished and knit together through its joints and ligaments, grows with a growth that is from God. [20] If with Christ you died to the elemental spirits of the world, why, as if you were still alive in the world, do you submit to regulations:[21] "Do not handle, do not taste, do not touch"[22] (referring to things that all perish as they are used)—according to human precepts and teachings?[23] These all have an appearance of wisdom in promoting self-made religion, asceticism, and severity to the body but are of no value in stopping indulgence of the flesh.

Even the commonly accepted doctrine of Confession to a priest has been misappropriated whereas the original context refers to sharing with one another for the purpose of mutual support. To do so communally would also prevent us from developing a holier than thou attitude towards one another.

James 5:16 Confess your sins one to another and pray one for another that you may be healed.

The lines prior to this admonition have been used, not just to try to justify the confessional booth but also, divine healing of physical disease. This is probably a good time to properly interpret the proper meaning of that.

I was called by my pastor on a number of occasions to speak on difficult issues. One time he called to request me to speak on the following sabbath regarding the fact a number of members had fallen ill, and a few others had actually died. I answered him in my usual style. "So, sir, my assumption is that you want me to make everyone feel good about this situation."

"Ah," he answered, "you understand me perfectly."

Imagine being put in that situation with but five days to prepare. It wasn't to be the only time I'd been tossed to the wolves. I called upon my "Barnabas" for research help, and he came through as usual.

"I've discovered something we've never noticed before," Jeff shouted out as he burst through the door. He was literally jumping about in excitement. Once I got him settled down, Jeff opened his Bible to the Epistle of James "Here in chapter five," he declared pointing to the verses which faith healers use to justify resisting medical aid, "it doesn't say what we've always assumed it does!"

[13]Is any among you afflicted? let him pray. Is any merry? let him sing psalms. [14]Is any sick among you? let him call for the elders of the church; and let them pray over him, anointing him with oil in the name of the Lord: [15]And the prayer of faith shall save the sick, and the Lord shall raise him up; and if he has committed sins, they shall be forgiven.

The actual language isn't about being sick, especially since the first verse the context is on emotional attitude. The proper translation refers to being "troubled of mind." In addition to illnesses so many had become troubled Jesus still had yet to return they required an anointing to establish we are under God's providence, James declares the troubled mind shall be settled. The troubling issue may still exist, but the troubled mind will be settled knowing God is in charge. Wow did that ever change things.

I went before the pulpit to express that; but, even more actionable, I showed how the infirm among us provide a service to the healthy by providing opportunities for prayer and service. One of our elders came to me afterwards and thanked me for explaining to him what exactly he was doing in such circumstances. He'd had no concept other than his efforts seemed always to be in vain. The end result was actually worse since those who God failed to heal were, then, accused of lacking in faith. The entire congregation seemed suddenly healthier.

Imagine: Another instance of God speaking through the mouth of a jackass! From that moment on, I've never been the same. That revelation got me looking more intensely into scripture. What else were we getting wrong about God? I began to visualize the poetic moment painted for us to interpret, and the reality of God's scriptural inspiration became apparent. I, also, came to realize the reason our 4th Century 'church fathers' sought so intensely to control the narrative.

This new heresy with which God had blessed me led to new adventures. I began to view scriptures that made little sense with a new eye. One that caught my attention had to do with the old saying, "Spare the rod and spoil the child." Was it allegorical, mis-interpreted, or an encouragement to beat our children with rods? Taking it literally didn't seem to improve behavior with prisons full of inmates who had been beaten, and universities populated by students who hadn't been.

Prov. 13:24 and 23:13-14 initially would seem to indicate that only sons, but not daughters, should be beaten. Girls back in the day must have been so much more well behaved. Upon further review we find the rod mentioned here is derived from the word **chevet**, that iconic curved shepherd's staff with which he directs, protects, and rescues his sheep. Something to keep in mind is how no shepherd ever beat his sheep. The reason they are caused to lay down beside the still waters is not that they have been beaten unconscious. Lord help the wolf that met up with the business end, however. It can as an effective defensive weapon.

In my understanding the poetic moment of Prov. 23:13-14 has to do with neglecting the proper instruction of our children. If you diligently instruct him, he will live. Also, in Prov.13:24, the poetic moment is "He who withholds instruction from a child is hating on him." After my congregation heard that message, they responded with relief induced applause.

The Bible is replete with many such examples. It becomes apparent the book we tend to wave about does not relate the inerrant Words of God even if the meaning behind them does. So, if it don't make sense, investigate. For, as the old song relates, "It ain't necessarily so."

CHAPTER EIGHT

HEAVEN OR HELL

I often hear the questioning television advertisement, "Are you going to go to heaven?" It always reminds me of an old joke wherein a pastor asks his congregation, "Raise your hand if you want to go to heaven." When one elderly lady didn't raise her hand, he asked, "why?"

"I thought you might be getting a group together for today," was her response.

While that may be worthy of a chuckle, it also raises up a further question. Where in the Bible does it say anything about the "saved" going to heaven when they die? Surprisingly, there is nothing in the Bible that promises such as our reward for following the Way of

Jesus. There are many scriptures that promise many things to followers of The Way, but none that specifically mention Heaven as our destination. On the contrary prophecies speak of God coming down to us from Heaven and dwelling here with us. (Rev. 21:1-27)

> [13]Brothers and sisters, we do not want you to be uninformed about those who sleep in death, so that you do not grieve like the rest of mankind, who have no hope. [14]For we believe that Jesus died and rose again, and so we believe that God will bring with Jesus those who have fallen asleep in him. [15] According to the Lord's word, we tell you that we who are still alive, who are left until the coming of the Lord, will certainly not precede those who have fallen asleep. [16] For the Lord himself will come down from heaven, with a loud command, with the voice of the archangel and with the trumpet call of God, and the dead in Christ will rise first. [17] After that, we who are still alive and are left will be caught up together with them in the clouds to meet the Lord in the air to forever be with the Lord . Therefore encourage one another with these words.

Please note, in this declaration, there is no mention of those who have died even hanging around "up yonder." Rather, the dead in Christ are to be raised from their graves on that day to join the returning Christ. As for any mention of the 'Rapture,' those Christians still alive at the return simply join in on the party. But, what then? Does He turn around and lead a procession back to heaven, or does he fulfill His promise and take possession of the creation?

> [21]Then I saw a new heaven and a new earth, for the old heaven and the old earth had passed away. And the sea was also gone. [2] And I saw the holy city, the new Jerusalem, coming down from God out of heaven like a bride beautifully dressed for her husband. [3] I heard a loud shout from the throne, saying, "Look, God's home is now among his people! He will live with them, and they will be his people. God himself will be with them.[a]

So, what about the rest of the dead? How does God deal with all those lost souls who, through whatever circumstance, never got the chance to know Jesus. Jesus' parable of the sheep and the goats seems to paint a dicey image of the condemned being separated from the blessed.

Matt 25:31 "When the Son of Man comes in his glory, and all the angels with him, he will sit on his glorious throne. [32] All the nations will be gathered before him, and he will separate the people one from another as a shepherd separates the sheep from the goats. [33] He will put the sheep on his right and the goats on his left. [41] "Then he will say to those on his left, 'Depart from me, you who are cursed, into the eternal fire prepared for the devil and his angels.

But is that the actual context here? Didn't we just see in Revelation that the blessed were already called up to join Christ at His return? So, then, just how and when is this 'judgement' taking place?

Rev. 20 And I saw an angel come down from heaven, having the key of the bottomless pit and a great chain in his hand. [2] And he laid hold on the dragon, that old serpent, which is the Devil, and Satan, and bound him a thousand years, [3] And cast him into the bottomless pit, and shut him up, and set a seal upon him, that he should deceive the nations no more, till the thousand years should be fulfilled: and after that he must be loosed a little season.

[4] Then I saw thrones, and they sat upon them, and judgment was given unto them: and I saw the souls of them that had been beheaded for the witness of Jesus, and for the Word of God, and which had not worshipped the beast, neither his image, neither had received his mark upon their foreheads, or in their hands; and they lived and reigned with Christ a thousand years. [5] But the rest of the dead lived not again until the thousand years were finished. This is the first resurrection. [6] Blessed and holy is he that hath part in the first resurrection: on such the second death hath no power, but they shall be priests of God and of Christ and shall reign with him a thousand years.

Whoa there, Nellie! A thousand years... first resurrection... the rest of the dead? This doesn't sound anything like what I was taught in Sunday School over cookies and Cool Aid.

[7] And when the thousand years are expired, Satan shall be loosed out of his prison, [8] And shall go out to deceive the nations which are in the four quarters of the earth, Gog, and Magog, to gather them together to battle: the number of whom is as the

sand of the sea.[9] And they went up on the breadth of the earth, and compassed the camp of the saints about, and the beloved city: and fire came down from God out of heaven, and devoured them.

Then after that, Jn. 5:28-29, the Age of Correction (Kolasin Aionion):

Rev. 20:12 And I saw the dead, small and great, stand before God; and the books were opened: and another book was opened, which is the book of life: and the dead were judged out of those things which were written in the books, according to their works.[13] And the sea gave up the dead in it; and death and hell delivered up the dead which were in them: and they were judged every man according to their works.

Who are all these people? They're, not only those lost souls whom missionaries sought to reach, but also those multitudes throughout history who have lived and died before the Word was even made available. These are all those who were believed to be cut off, ignorant of the truth of the almighty God of creation. St. Augustine pondered over how and why the vast majority of humanity refused to answer such an obvious altar call. He erroneously presumed God was only interested in a special few… that He had predetermined whom He would save while condemning the great mass of humanity to damnation. It was the genesis of the satanic doctrine of Calvinism which inspired John Calvin to portray the image of an angry God dangling sinners by a slender thread over burning hellfire.

But wait! In these next scriptures we are relieved to learn God has had a happy ending planned from the very beginning, and He's sticking to it. And notice, in verse 45, how the books (bibles) will be opened, and they (the newly resurrected) will be judged (taught) from out of them. Here's a hint: Former president Harry Truman first served as a county judge. However, he did so without having earned a Law Degree because County Judge was an administrative position devoted to managing the affairs of the county, such as garbage collection and road maintenance. So, the Kingdom of God is to be, likewise, 'judged,' but not by a justice of the peace.

In John 6:44-48 Jesus answered them, "No one can come to Me unless the Father who sent Me draws them, and I will raise them up on the last day. It is written in the Prophets, 'And they will all be taught by God.'"

Gal 6:20 And when the world, that shall begin to vanish away, shall be finished, then will I shew these tokens: t**he books shall be opened before the firmament**, and they shall see all together:

Rev. 20:12 And I saw the dead, small and great, standing before God, and the books were opened. And another book was opened, which is the Book of Life. And the dead were judged accordingly.

It would seem our loving God has had a plan all along to save, not just the few, but all humanity. How, then, can the following assertion be answered?

Luke 23:43 "And Jesus said unto him, "Verily I say unto thee, today shalt thou be with me in paradise." The original Greek was written without punctuation, and the early translators punctuated their translation, improperly. Since Jesus spent three days and three nights in the tomb, how could He have been in heaven with the thief that very day? Now, however, a bit of editing completely changes the meaning. "Verily I say to you today, you shall be with me in Paradise."

Note, also, He didn't say heaven. A few other questions arise as follows:

In my Father's house there are many habitations

This relates to how open God's grace is to all, not which bed & breakfast room will be assigned. We've already seen His dwelling will be on earth.

Matthew 6:19 Lay not up for yourselves treasures upon earth, where moth and rust doth corrupt, and where thieves break through and steal:

Obviously, this relates to where our focus should be in this temporary life. A final argument for the heaven/hell argument relates a parable of the rich man and the beggar. After they both die, the rich msn observes the poor man bring cared for by Abraham. From his grave he begs Abraham to allow him to warn his brothers to change their ways. Abraham predicts how Jesus will be rejected by his own people. As with all of the parables, this was narrated to express a lesson to his disciples "who had an ear to hear."

Luke 1:30 But he said to him, 'If they do not listen to Moses and the Prophets, they will not be persuaded even if someone rises from the dead.'"

OK, as pointed out the 'saved' don't actually go to heaven. What about all those icky bad actors? What does the Bible say about them?

Rev 20:10 the devil that deceived them was cast into the lake of fire and brimstone, where the beast and the false prophet are, and shall be tormented day and night till the end of time (aeonium).

Matt 13 [14] And death and hell were cast into the lake of fire. This is the second death. [15] And whosoever was not found written in the book of life was cast into the lake of fire.

This indicates the fate of those who refuse to accept the free gift of Grace will simply be consumed and exist no more. Why anyone would resist such mercy is far beyond my paygrade. So, in retrospect let's review what I hope we are beginning to 'GET about God.'

1: Creation can be as old as you'd like, thus allowing the eternal designer to create the coal and oil deposits humanity will need.

2: God is not constrained by 'time.'

3: The Bible was ordained as the rule book of the corporate church centuries after Christ. Therefore, do not mulishly follow the words but interpret the poetic meaning God intends.

4: Its Poetic Moment is still of value to our understanding.

5: Heaven is not the reward of the saved and will eventually be done away with.

6: Eternal death, not punishment is the alternative

7: All humanity, with but a few possible exceptions, will qualify. The plan, boss, the plan!

So, what went wrong? How is it the journey of "going to church" has jumped so far off the original tracks? Read on about the true bread of life.

CHAPTER NINE

THE EKKLESIA

Where is the true church of God? Jesus proclaimed, "I will build my church and the gates of hell shall not withstand it." There is that really humongous world dominating one based in Rome, but there are numerous off-shoots and independent sects scattered all about the landscape. Is it all of them combined? Is it any single one of these? But if one of them is correct, then all the others must, as a result, be in error. So, is it none of them? While we cannot all be right, we could all be wrong. However, if you are a believer, then it would seem at least one of them must be hiding out there like Waldo is, doesn't it? So, then, where IS Waldo?

While I may not know where Waldo is hiding, I have learned where God be hanging out, and it's not in an altar built by mortal hands. His dwelling place is amongst the **Ecclesia**; "those called by Him to a purpose."

Ephesians 2:22: "in whom you also are being built together into a dwelling of God in the Spirit," And Luke 17:20; The kingdom of God is within you.

I was reading a truly powerful book, **Tattoos on the Heart** by Gregory Boyle a Catholic priest, when I received a revelation from a quote by Teilhard de Chardin, "Trust in the slow work of God. *Ours is a God who waits. It takes what it takes for the great turn around. Who are we not to do so as well? Wait for it.*"

Jesus proclaimed, "You are the light of the world." As Fr. Boyle adds, "He did not say, **one day if you are more perfect and try really hard, you'll be light, or if you play by the rules, then maybe you'll become light**. No, He states straight out, *You ARE the light*. It is the truth of who you are, waiting only for you to discover it."

This expresses so well how my concept of God's plan for ALL humanity began to take form following a traumatic experience over two decades ago.

I was the scheduled speaker at *The Pacific Garden Mission* on the South side of Chicago when God got my attention. My soon to be ex-pastor had recommended me to them. As he had put it, "Bill, I believe you have a message they need to hear. But keep in mind these are street people attending in order to receive a free meal, so you'll have to do something to grab their attention right off the bat."

Little did I know he was setting me up. I'm still not clear on what message it was he believed would be well received. We never had the promised preliminary discussion since His promise to guide me through the intimidating process was reneged upon as I was on my way to our meeting at the mission.

"Sorry, Bill, but something unexpected has come up and I won't be able to join you. But you'll do fine," he assured me as he provided me with a quick briefing. "Just remember, most of these guys are drugged up and only putting up with you as the price of a free meal. You'll need to say something to grab their attention right off, or you'll lose the lot of them." I pulled up at their South State Street location facing what is generally regarded as the greatest of human fears: public speaking. *God help me, how did I ever get roped into this?*

As I approached the pulpit, after being auspiciously introduced as "the man of god," I took a moment to silently scan the sea of faces staring me down. It was a racially mixed mélange of beaten down humanity. I could feel the despair, the lack of hope for anything beyond the latest fix. How could I reach them with what little I had to offer. Obviously, they'd heard it all before.

It was now more than obvious what Pastor Richard had meant with his instruction to grab their attention right from the git go. My original opening was discarded as was my preconceived message. This was to be no *Sermon on the Mount*. What could I say? One thing came to mind. After an overly pregnant moment of indecision, I dove in with my initial impression of their overall state of being.

"LIFE SUCKS!" I bellowed out from the base of my gut. "But then," I finished in a softer sarcastic tone, "you don't need Whitey coming up here to tell you that, do you?"

I had their attention!!!

"Do God BE all-mighty?" I asked using the Ebonese term, BE, indicating a constant unending action finding its way through my tongue.

"Amen," was the surprising response. We seemed to have achieved a connection.

"Do God BE all-knowing?" I added.

"Amen!"

"Do God BE all-loving?" I continued.

"AMEN!"

It was as if I was being fed the right words to share. "Then God BE knowing you. In fact, He BE who put you on the tracks you be on. Since He BE in total control, He BE responsible for what you BE dealing with. Therefore, He has already forgiven you before you were even born, He BE forgiving you ever after, AMEN!"

"AMEN,": came back at me like a resounding echo down a winding canyon.

I was charged with emotion and the formerly lost congregation was getting into it right along with me. Empowered by their energy, I went on to further proclaim how, despite feeling beyond the Grace of God, they were the most valued of all. They represented the very lost souls Jesus had hung with. Now, since they had already been forgiven, all that was left for them to do was accept that totally free gift of grace, forgive themselves, and then one another. What we all needed more than anything else was to hug one another as God was hugging us all together.

At this point, the Master Pastor jumped up waving his arms and totally crying out, "No more, no more! I've heard enough." I was ordered to stand down from the pulpit.

"But…" I stuttered in shock. "Let me finish. I have an important point to make."

"No, young man, I will not have this nonsense… about hugging of all things… in my house." he commanded with a jerk of his thumb like an umpire dramatically calling me out for trying to steal home plate. He was apoplectic.

"No, no," the crowd shouted back. "Let the man speak! Let the man speak!"

Humoring myself by imagining all the crimson shades through which Master Pastor must have passed through before erupting like Mt. St. Helens, I calmed myself and turned back to settle the congregation. "The pastor is correct. This be HIS house with HIS rules, and I must comply. However," I finished as he closed on me, "despite that fact, God still BE here sitting down there amongst you. So, remember that you all BE forgiven and loved by your Heavenly Father.

Nobody can take that away from you. Now come forward," I added referencing the coming altar call, "and BE healed." Then, feeling alone and sorely deflated, I allowed myself to be escorted away.

As I left the chapel, though, I passed by a particularly intimidating fellow with a scared face. He had seemed to ignore me throughout the entire service; but, as I passed by, we locked eyes together and I was gifted with a slight nod, an acknowledgement I most craved at that otherwise dark moment in time. Then, as I sat alone in the ante' room, I could hear the pastor encouraging members of the congregation to come forward. It was obviously a successful altar call.

Before I left the Mission, the pastor accused me of taking a condescending attitude to the assemblage. It later occurred to me that Jesus had been constantly accused of the very same thing, condescending to hang out and eat with sinners. Unfortunately, I failed to think of that till later. It wouldn't have mattered, though. What did matter was what was happening within me as a direct result of this experience. It was a slowly developing realization that the churches of this world were working contrary to what Jesus had proclaimed, "Know ye not that ye are gods?" As in Caiaphas' statement in *Corpus Christi*, they needed sinners, not gods.

Instead, I told El Pastor how I had been following the example of the Apostle Paul in being "all things to all men that by all means I might reach a few" He explained the message they desired was a sort of **Calvinist** 'gospel of success.' In other words, I had been expected to give witness to how my obedience to God had led to being blessed with worldly success. Had I been aware of that in advance I would have declined the offer to give such a false witness. Faith in God had seen me through many a difficult scrape, which had been my original speech plan.

However, my life had been far from a financial success. My old minister had been well aware of that and set me up for the fall because he wanted the "Street" to hear a message of perseverance without suffering any personal blowback. I can only imagine what must have come back to him over my ultimate bait and switch, because I never again returned to attend church. Twenty years later, at a funeral on the South Side, I heard I had achieved fame amongst the homies with that simple message of hope. So, ultimately it had been worth the emotional trauma, not to mention how the blowback from that moment of epiphany totally changed the trajectory of my belief structure towards Unitarian concepts. God works patiently. Consider how long it took to convert those huge prehistoric creatures and plants into the resources modern society depends upon. Wait for it!

That same, soon to become an ex-minister for me, is the very one who had once challenged me to write this book. Today I forgive him. It was all b'shert! He had no more say in his actions than did Pharaoh dealing with Moses. As I finish this chapter, I cannot help but visualize the homies described by Fr. Boyle and how the only thing most of them needed was to be believed in. Fr. Boyle refers to it as the Japanese term **amae**, living in the deep sense of being cherished. Compassion isn't just about feeling the pain of others; it's about bringing them in towards yourself. If we love what God loves, then margins get erased. To be compassionate as God is, means dismantling any barriers that exclude.

What is it the churches of this world teach? That we are all hopeless sinners in need of redemption... that we are damned and destined to suffer in hell UNLESS... John Calvin once described our creator as an angry old man suspending us over the fires of Hell by the slenderest of threads and just begging for an excuse to send us to an eternity of suffering. In order to EARN the 'free gift' of grace, He demands penitence through a variety of acts of contrition. We are, apparently so far-gone God had to sacrifice his only son to redeem us. We are offered forgiveness only IF we accept the sacrifice of Jesus – a free gift with conditions.

However, in viewing the passionate prayer of Jesus questioning the need for His crucifixion prior to His arrest in the Garden of Gethsemane, (Luke 22;42 *"Father, if thou be willing, remove this cup from me")* the question of just who it was that actually required it is raised. Was it the all-powerful God, or was it a population used to blood sacrifices as a sin offering who actually needed to see blood shed before they would begin to believe they had actually been forgiven? Just sayin'… Seems to this thankful sinner, that would put even more value on such a sacrifice.

In addition, what about the vast sea of humanity for whom this ostensibly free gift has never been available? Whether through cultural resistance or simply having lived and died prior to Jesus, how does God deal with them? Does a loving God write them off as irredeemable? Being blind to the ultimate plan of creation, St. Augustine, among others like John Calvin , concluded such must be so.

Those characters listening to me pontificating had generally felt themselves beyond redemption. The lives of many of them were colored by the idea, "since I'm already too sinful to be acceptable, why even bother to try? I might as well just go out and be as bad as I can be!" As a direct result, acting out was the likely result. But that was not the deity I wanted to reveal to them. My desire had been to declare the all-inclusive Eternal YHVH who sees them as they are each destined to BE-come.

For this sin, I had been shut down by the resident berobed gatekeeper. But why? apparently the true message of grace reduced authority over his flock. He was their contact with God as, in the play, *Corpus Christi*, when Judas asks High Priest Caiaphas, "Why did you have to kill Jesus? Was it because he said He was God?"

"No," the high priest had replied, "it was because He said you were all gods. We need sinners, not gods."

But, of course, just like a fish needs water and the World Health Authority needed Covid, priests need sinners. Jesus tore the symbolic curtain separating the Holy of Holies from we common sinners. The priesthood was no longer necessary. Jesus, as the new high priest, now made is possible to go straight to YHVH with our prayers. Is it any wonder Catholic and Jewish services have so much in common?

Protestant services don't usually go to such extremes, but the separation between the ordained and laity is still evident. In most cases the emphasis is on the difference between the righteous and sinners, giving rise to an us against them attitude. The bright shining difference of works like **Homeboy Industries** shames the Sunday go to worship crowd. How could this pious pastor accuse me of condescending to his congregation? The entire ministry of Jesus had been condescending. He had been under constant accusation of condescending to eat and hang out with sinners. Is it any wonder Jesus charges the self-righteous of our society with the following:"

[7] "Judge not, that you be not judged. [2] For with the judgment you pronounce you will be judged, and with the measure you use it will be measured to you. [3] Why do you see the speck that is in your brother's eye, but do not notice the log that is in your own eye? [4] Or how can you say to your brother, 'Let me take the speck out of your eye,' when there is the log in your own eye? [5] You hypocrite, first take the log out of your own eye, and then you will see clearly to take the speck out of your brother's eye.

[21] "Not everyone who says to me, 'Lord, Lord,' will enter the kingdom of heaven, but the one who does the will of my Father who is in heaven. [22] On that day many will say to me, 'Lord, Lord, did we not prophesy in your name, and cast out demons in your name, and do many mighty works in your name?' [23] And then will I declare to them, 'I never knew you; depart from me, you workers of lawlessness. For in as much as you did thus to the least of my brethren, ye did so to me."

In everything, then, do to others as you would have them do to you. For this is the essence of the Law and the Prophets. **Galatians 5:14** The entire law is fulfilled in a single decree: "Love your neighbor as yourself."

That's how to find the true church those called to fulfill the Law and the prophets. The ecclesia of Jesus is not contained within a physical cathedral or even a steepled building. It's a spiritual body wherever those called to that purpose are gathered. For, "wherever two or more of you are gathered in my name, there I am with you." This revelation has caused me to review my entire belief structure. It was, in fact, the impetus that has resulted as the motivation for the studies that have led to the writing of this very book.

YHVH is so much greater than we can even imagine. No wonder we have been commanded not to attempt to portray (unknowable adjective) a craven image of anything related to the spiritual world... We are only just now getting close to being able to imagine what it is we cannot yet imagine.

Chew on that for now.

CHAPTER TEN

LEAVENING THE LOAVES

So, just how have the churches of this world been derailed? Well, first, as I have previously pointed out I am not a Biblical Scholar. I'm merely an example of how God can still get His point across through the big mouth of a Balaam's jackass. But I AM a poet so, while struggling how best to relate the way in which corporate Christianity has ****** up the simplicity of Jesus, I have spent a lot of time praying for an effective allegory. The following is what has been given in answer:

Back when Jesus and the disciples...heh, Jesus and the Disciples sounds a lot like either a Chicago street gang or an 80's grunge band doesn't it? It reminds me of a blog piece I once did picturing Jesus and the Disciples thundering into Jerusalem on their Harleys and stirring up the dust on the temple mount. Well, that is sort'a what they did, ain't it?

Getting back to the point, Jesus and his disciples were about to head out across the Sea of Galilee to start a new gig of some sort and one of them commented, "Hey we forgot to pack lunch." Well, it was something to the effect that, "we didn't bring bread." They were, then, probably expecting Jesus to "miracle" up a basket of loaves and fishes. Instead, He turned to them in his usual allegorical manner and proclaimed, "Beware the leaven of the Pharisees and the Sadducees."

"What the... is He...?" They got to waving arms about, "warning us about now? Is He upset that we might grab the wrong kind of bread?

Jesus looked at them and asked. "How many times do I have to 'splain things to you guys? Don't you ever get it? I'm talking about the Pharisees and the leaven which they've kneaded into all their religious schmutz from which I am come to free you." Suddenly the guys got it!!! Sort of.

We were taking in the recent coronation of the new English king when my companion commented, "This

I so over the top that it reminds me of a high Catholic mass... excluding maybe the swinging of incense lamps but with all the other paraphernalia and ceremonial schmutz." Then I thought back to all the pomp and circumstance associated with the 2nd Ecumenical Council of the Roman Church which had been designed to bring "all the churches into one accord."

At that moment the concept of the poetic moment became clear to me, as well. It had been apparent to me how Jesus wasn't referring to bread. It had even been obvious how He was referring to all the pomp and circumstance with which a self-aggrandizing priesthood clothes itself. But it went so much deeper than that, and He could foresee what was to be. What suddenly took form is what prompted me to step beyond my personal blind faith acceptance of a false reality which had been pulled over my eyes.

The Blue Pill or the Red Pill?

Around 70 A.D. "Rome burned while Nero fiddled." The emperor needed a scapegoat with which to deflect accusations that he was to blame for the huge conflagration. The Jewish Zealots and anyone else associated with the radicals rebelling against Roman rule provided the perfect target. The resultant purge of all things remotely associated resulted in the destruction of the Jewish temple and slaughter of the population of Jerusalem as well as the martyrdom of Peter, Paul, and any other adherents to *The Way* who had not already split the scene. These martyrs now provided a seemingly unending supply of entertainment for the masses in the Colosseum. The "time and times" of the Great Tribulation continued on and off for the next three centuries.

Just try to grasp that: three centuries of limited interaction amongst the faithful, many of whom took up residence in the Catacombs below Rome itself. Think about how much has changed for us between 1700 A.D. and the past century even in the form of government. Is it any surprise that, somehow, somewhere along the way the "simplicity that is in Christ Jesus," as taught by Paul, was lost and redefined by those robes still motivated to exercise a semblance of control?

The ***Ecclesia*** (Greek for those individuals "called to a purpose") were quickly steamrolled by a corporate church complete with priests and bishops and, eventually Popes, Cardinals, and the Office of the Inquisition to control doctrine and silence contrary opinions. Following Constantine's ***Edict of Milan***, the soon-to-be State Religion of the Holy Roman Empire, as visualized by Emperor Constantine and established by Theodosius in A.D. 381, that emerged from hiding bore little resemblance to the little flock of Jesus.

The general focus upon those authorities seeking unity was the need for an instruction manual. It was decreed that a Holy Bible should be constructed and a council for that purpose was selected.

But who was to select and compile such sacred words? These guys couldn't even agree on the nature of their chief subject of the Nicaean Council without acting out of character. The Septuagint, Greek translations of the Jewish scriptures, had been compiled some 300 years prior to the incarnation of Jesus. Those, along with the various letters written by Paul and the other 1st century evangelists were the only reference works available to the early church. There were contrary messages even then, though, as previously warned about by Paul: Col. 2:8,18.

Beware lest any man spoil you through philosophy and vain deceit, after the tradition of men, the rudiments of the world, and not after Christ...

Even such leaders as Peter, Paul, and James the Just maintained vehement differences of opinion on what it meant to be a follower of The Way. By the time Constantine had called the Council of Nicaea to order there were literally hundreds of versions of the Gospel, so it's easy to comprehend how the message of Jesus could have become muddled.

Early Christian writings greatly outnumbered the 27 books that would become the canon of the New Testament. The "shepherds of the Church," by a process of spiritual discernment and investigation into the liturgical traditions of the Church sought to draw clear lines of distinction between books they agreed to be truly inspired by God and originated in the apostolic period, and those which only claimed to have these qualities. No doubt, a significant amount of "horse trading" took place: "Give us James; we'll accept Timothy. At least tobacco hadn't yet been introduced into the atmosphere.

The process culminated in 382 at the Council of Rome. The biblical canon was reaffirmed by the regional councils of Hippo (393) and Carthage (397), and

definitively reaffirmed by the ecumenical Council of Florence in 1442.

Finally, the ecumenical Council of Trent solemnly defined this same canon in 1546, after it came under attack by the first Protestant leaders, including Martin Luther.

Different denominations recognized different lists of books as canonical, following various church councils and the decisions of leaders of various churches. Even the Ten Commandments were subject to editing by the Roman Catholic Church as shown below. Note the change between command numbers 2-4 and 9-10 between the two versions. Why do you suppose that might be so?

Ten Commandments
Exodus 20:1-17 KJV

1: I am the Lord your God. You shall have no other gods before me. Note this does not preclude the existence of lesser gods.

2: <u>You shall not make unto thee any graven</u> image of anything that is in heaven above, nor on the ground below or that is in the waters below that you should <u>bow down to nor worship them</u>. *Thus, diminishing the glory of what we cannot perceive.*

3: You shall not take the name of the Lord your God in vain for the lord your God will not hold such blameless. *Teaching or behaving contrary to the Way of God.*

4: Remember the Sabbath day to keep it holy.

5: Honor your father and mother that your days upon the earth may be long

6: You shall not kill. *Do no murder.*

7: You shall not commit adultery.

8: You shall not steal.

9: You shall not bear false witness against your neighbor.

10: You shall not covet your neighbor's house, nor his wife, nor his servants, nor his ox, nor anything else that is thy neighbor's property.

Next follows the Catholic version of the big Ten. Other than minor variations in the text note the <u>total elimination of the second commandment against idols</u> and the splitting up of the tenth commandment into two separate ones to make up for the edited-out 2nd missive. Which do you believe to be correct and which an example of Jesus' warning to 'beware the leaven of the Pharisees? So much for the literal inerrant divine nature of scripture.

1: I am the Lord your God. You shall worship the Lord your God and Him only shall you serve.

2: You shall not take the name of the Lord your God in vain.

3: Remember to keep holy the Sabbath day.

4: Honor your father and mother.

5: You shall not kill.

6: You shall not commit adultery.

7: You shall not steal.

8: You shall not bear false witness against your neighbor.

9: You shall not covet your neighbor's wife.

10: You shall not covet your neighbor's goods.

I find it deeply troubling that an event as iconic as the presentation of the Ten Commandments can be so blatantly twisted by the established representatives there-of! What else might the leaven of our trusted shepherds be guilty of? Fool me once, shame on you. Fool me twice, shame on me.

Where then does that leave us? If that great big, massive assembly is not the true unleavened church, what is? Does it even exist? Has the antichrist won? Jesus promised He would build His church and the grave would not prevail against it, so where is it? Am I simply trying to lure you off to another? Am I, as in an old Flip Wilson routine laughed about, attempting to set up *the Church of What's Happening Now?*

While my fellow conspirator in heresy has grown up through the Catholic traditions, I haven't. As a result, one might expect me to go off in praise of Martin Luther and the Protestant Reformation. While I might identify with his initial motivation, Luther eventually got caught up in that Pharisaical leavening process, as well. The followers of John Wesley could well attest to that. As mentioned in my author intro, I grew up in and through an Evangelical Bible Church. However, when I raised certain questions to my pastor, to put it simply, I was advised to simply 'pay and pray' and leave such issues to the experts.

Until my wife died and I nearly followed close behind, I drifted from fellowship to fellowship hoping to find God's Gee Spot. But I didn't die. God simply removed all incumbrances of normal life and set me up in a wilderness of contemplation. At long last, free to focus on the meaning of life, much has become apparent to me. Where is the ecclesia, the true calling of Jesus? I have discovered it dwelling within me…and possibly you, as well since you've read this far in search of truth.

Jesus said it: Luke 17:20-22 And when he was demanded of the Pharisees, when the kingdom of God should come, he answered them and said, "The kingdom of God cometh not with observation: [21] Neither shall they say, Lo here! or, lo there! for, behold, the kingdom of God is within you."

Jn. 14:6 Jesus said, "I am the Way, the Truth, and the Light. No one comes to the father except through me."

That being realized for what it means, the following scripture explaining why so many get caught up by the schmutz of all that leaven, provides the basis of chapter 11.

John. 6:24 No man can come to me except the Father who has sent me first draw him to me.

CHAPTER ELEVEN

IS GOD TRYING TO SAVE THIS WORLD?

So, again comes the question, what is God up to? All sorts of commentary has dealt with this over the years. Is God dead? Has he gone off on vacation or to the privy? Did He get things started only to step aside to dispassionately observe the results? Or is it, as certain of the Gnostic heresy have proposed, that there are two equal gods; a good god that rules heaven and an evil one who has created and rules this world? Or is it all, as Pope Leo X stated, "a financially advantageous fable?" I guess it's time to prove the IS of our Creator.

How does one prove the fact of something invisible to our mortal existence? Does the concept of existence even apply to God who IS beyond the limits of time and space? For the sake of discussion let us simply go with exists.

How do we know there is air? John 3:8 ***The wind blows where it listeth and you cannot see from where it comes or where it goes. So is everything that is of the spirit.*** By itself we cannot see, smell, or taste it. However, we can observe its effects. We can both feel and see the results of the wind. We can compress air and use it to lift or power objects. We can do the same with God by observing the results of divine design. If I seem to go overboard with the following examples of how God signs His name, please excuse me. This is so important; it has to be knocked out of the park.

We've already seen how the Bible allows for the universe to be any age science wants to call it. That also means the hypothesis of evolution can subsume all the time it needs to develop the vast array of plants and creatures which have died eons ago and turned to coal and oil. Take all the time evolution requests; I still don't see how lizards jumping out of trees could ever evolve the ability to fly. The first time any number of lizards hit the ground, that would preclude any additional attempts. Study the design of a feather. It is so much more complex than a scale.

Beyond the amazing complexity of feathers, the rest of avian design requires hollow bones and their distinctly un-reptilian high metabolism. Just because they sort of resemble each other from a safe distance, chickens are not related to Tyrannosaurus Rex!

While we're on the subject of our fine feathered friends, consider the seasonal journeys of the Arctic Tern. This champion traveler makes the journey from Arctic to Antarctic regions and back every year. How do it know? What motivated the first Tern to begin its initial migration, and how did it know where to go and when to leave? It had to be successful, or it would not have survived to tell the tale.

Before you suggest the obvious answer, I already know that argument. One would think the birds would take note of the dwindling of their food supply and begin moving with the seasons. That makes total sense. It's, also, a total error. The silly birds begin the seasonal migration right at the very moment their food supply is at its greatest. By doing so, they arrive at the opposite polar region at the very moment their food supply becomes available there. Like our body hair, how DO it know? Who programmed them?

While this conundrum festers in the background, here are a few other creation anecdotes to serve up as appetizers. Way back when the rotating gas clouds began to congeal and form the stars and related planets, all those great gaseous clouds of matter rotated uniformly, right? They began as a few big masses of gasses that broke up (how & why?) into smaller individuals still spinning and slowly congealing. That's the theory of how our Solar System formed. That being the case, how come everything in our Solar System rotates in the same direction except for Venus which rotates in the opposite direction: God messing with us?

Then we have the conundrum of water and ice. All liquids shrink when they solidify; or expand as they heat and liquify. If ice and water followed this rule of nature, no life would be possible. As water would freeze it would sink to the bottom. Eventually life would be choked off. But the designer of our universe foresaw this and created an exception to the rule like aye before before eee, except after cee . In the moment just before water freezes, it stops contracting and expands just enough to make ice lighter than water to that it will float instead of sink. If not so, the seas would have become ice choked from the bottom on up. Only water does that.

Our God possesses the ultimate sense of humor, as well. Ever studied ducks? How can you not laugh? Unless you're a hunter, that is. Then you just smile and rack up a round. Beyond that, we have the duckbilled platypus, a critter so strange that botanists thought the first one they received had been sewn together as a joke. Not only is it an egg laying mammal, from its radar sensory duck bill to its poison clawed rear webbed feet, it's a living exception to the rules…why?

Included in that gallery of weirdness are creatures like archer fish that spit bugs out of the air, Angler fish that have a fishing lure built out from their noses, and deep-sea creature features with their own private lighting systems. Then, as a whale of a tale, God designed ocean mammals such as dolphins and toothed whales to give birth tail first. These air breathing fellows birth their offspring that way so they do not drown during the struggle as they would if they had to fight their way out headfirst like every other mammalian critter.

Everywhere we look the hand of the Designer is apparent. Whether in the perfectly engineered tilt of the earth to provide us with manageable seasons, the gravitational pull of the Moon stirring the tides which keep the seas from stagnation, and the ionosphere which protects us from the Sun's harmful radiation God's design is apparent. Add to all that the apparently limitless canopy of stars above us to keep ourselves centered, and the hand of the Creator is obvious. So, as Jesus cried out, 'my God, my God, why hast thou abandoned me?!" Why does it so often feel like we've been abandoned?

Have we, or is the problem with our perceptions? Are we guilty of forgetting to remove our fingers from the send button of our spiritual microphone? What might God be up to? What might we hear if we ask the right questions and let go of that send button? What might we take in if we dim the blinding lights of our so-called civilization that prevent us from beholding the limitless stars above?

The account of Pentecost in Acts 2:1–11 emphasizes that people from all over the world heard simple Galileans speaking in the pilgrims' individual languages after the descent of heavenly fire and wind. The theological message became evident: God was intent on putting an end of all exclusive and elitist religion. His loving gift of Grace was spread out to all humanity, and their little doggies, too. Am I being ridiculous? SELAH Don't all dogs go to heaven? I hope so, and this is from a cat servant.

Shortly afterwards Paul began his ministry to the Greek gentiles. He was followed shortly there-after by Peter and the other apostles. But it's a big world. Would God be content with that? What of the rest of His creation?

How does a parent teach a child not to touch the hot stove? You can warn the kid all you want; but, until he/she actually gets burned, the lesson is only vaguely theoretical. The trick is in managing any such lessons so as to limit potential damage. Humanity has been born into a world full of "hot stoves." We've been given all sorts of warnings against burning ourselves. Should God have supernaturally prevented us from burning ourselves, what would we have learned? And it's an interactive experience. We have to learn the lessons to-gether. Fortunately, God's Grace protects us from the potential of eternal harm.

As Father Richard Rohr of the **Institute for Contemplation** has written,

- Neither sin nor salvation could ever be exclusive-ly mine, but both of them are collectively *ours*!
- Universal solidarity is the important lesson, not private salvation.
- *Human solidarity* is the goal, not "my" moral su-periority or perfection.

I know that doesn't at first feel like a strategy for successful living, and it is certainly not one that will ever appeal to the upwardly mobile or pure idealists. It first feels like capitulation, but that is not Jesus' or Paul's intention at all—quite the opposite. Paul believes he has found a new kind of victory and freedom. He himself calls it "folly" or "foolishness" (1 Corinthians 1:21, 25, 27; 4:10), as it is for most people to this day. He often calls it a "hidden mystery" that only the wise discover. Paul believes there is a hidden, cruciform shape to reality, even revealed in the geometry of the cross (see Ephesians 2:13–22). The world is filled with contradictions, false alternatives, zero-sum games, paradoxes, and unresolvable evils. It is foundationally unjust, yet we must work for justice in order to find our own freedom and create it for others of all creeds and ethnicities.

Paul is an utter realist about life on this planet. We must fully recognize and surrender to this foundational reality before we try to think we can repair the world (*tikkun olam* in Hebrew) with freedom and love. Paul's insight is symbolized in the scandalous image of a man on the cross, the Crucified God who fully accepts and transforms this tragic human situation through love. If this is the reality to which even God must submit, then surely, we must and can do the same." *Richard Rohr (The Institute for Contemplative Study)*

That is why I believe God has gone to all the work, including the prehistorical geological preparations, to build this world as an interactive exercise in growing to our potential. With all its flaws, pain, and beauty, we learn to respect and navigate through the perplexing array of hot stoves tempting our eager fingers. And not all will GET it on this go-around. But stay tuned. That's been worked into the warp and woof of life's fabric, as well.

CHAPTER TWELVE

RECESS TIME

After all the heavy lifting of the previous chapters, before I attempt to explore God's end game, I feel it is time to have a little fun with scriptural confusion. As should be apparent by now, I do not subscribe to the notion of all the Bible being the inerrant literal words of God. Instead, I think of it as Mankind's words with which we attempt to explain the poetic moment our Creator is attempting to share with us. That being the case, we can expound upon any number of cases in which one scripture not only contradicts another, but where some miss the point of it altogether.

My key hook in this activity has already been dealt with in the Genesis 1:1-3 beginning of creation narrative allowing for billions and billions of stars existing for billions and billions of years as well as the fossilized evidence of previous creations. That's an example of where the simple mistranslation of the original text can totally skew anything further pondered upon.

I've recently pointed out how the Catholic Bible eliminated the admonition against the use of religious idols in worship and broke up the tenth commandment into two separate line items so as to preserve the sacred number at ten, but we have the same sort of issue with the observance of Easter.

One of the main issues dealt with at Nicaea, but not resolved, had to do with setting the date for a uniform observance of the resurrection narrative. But alas, since the Roman and Eastern Orthodox Churches were unable to agree upon which calendar, the Julian or Gregorian, in which to set the date Jesus has ever since been forced to endure two separate crucifixions each year. Beyond that there's the problem of counting three days and three nights between sundown Friday and sunrise Sunday. I'll explain that little math matter later on at the conclusion of this chapter.

But next let's take a look at certain itchy issues related to adherents of the faith. I think we've all heard, at one time or another, of a sick child whose family refuses to accept medical treatment relying, instead, upon a faith healer. On occasion such children overcome the illness and the family proclaims hallelujah! But all too often the child suffers unnecessarily. The involved parties are often declared to be lacking in faith thereby compounding feelings of guilt. In addition, it's tough enough when the parties in need of divine healing happen to be adults. It is, after all, their choice to do so. But, when a helpless child is involved, it's a different matter ALTOGETHER. God best helps those with the ability to help themselves.

Now, having an idea of the power of prayer, I don't doubt that some have experienced faith healing. I've done so myself. One instance dealt with my Jewish daughter-in-law who was suffering from Crohn's Disease. Prior to her surgery I appealed to my pastor to pray for her healing. He was hesitant to do so without her personally requesting it, but I persisted. The following day, when she was being prepped the doctors could find no evidence of the disease. It caused no end to consternation followed by cancellation of the procedure.

Sometime later, in the midst of an argument, she declared, "You don't give a damn about me and never have!"

I countered with, "That's not true. When you were due for your surgery I spent the entire night praying for you... not that it matters to you."

That stopped her cold. "Don't be so certain. Something happened that nobody could explain,' was her response. The argument was also cured.

All too often, however, the prayer for healing seems to go unanswered. Then the physical issue is compounded with the emotional distress of, "If only your faith were stronger..." The point I wish to make has to do with the mis-translated scriptures used to support the practice.

One auspicious Monday I received a call from my minister requesting that I speak on the following Sabbath Day with the observation, "Bill, we've had a few members die recently, and even more have become ill."

"And," I answered back, "you want me to get up in the pulpit and make everyone feel good about it, right?"

"You understand perfectly," was his predictable answer. I was his go to gunslinger for handling any issue he didn't feel comfortable dealing with.

My initial concept was to show the valuable service a member provided by presenting prayer material and service ops to the rest of the congregation. On its own that narrative would have done the job. However, the answer my study buddy presented to me changes the entire justification for what faith healers, most of whom are sincere, pontificate about. It has nothing to do with curing the common aches, illnesses, and injuries common to life. It has to do with pulling on your big boy pants and "getting over it." The standard issue text is as follows:

> James 5:14 Is anyone among you sick? Let them call the elders of the church to lay hands on them and anoint them with oil in the name of the Lord. 15 And the prayer offered in faith will make the sick person well.

"The Greek word used here," Jeff explained practically jumping up and down with excitement, "is **choleh** and it's better translated as '***troubled of mind***.' The verse is better rendered as 'are any amongst you troubled of mind? Let them go to the elders and have hands laid upon them and praying over them and their troubled minds shall be set at ease.

Now it is easy to imagine how badly the early followers of Jesus Christ would be troubled of mind.

Everyone, including Paul and the rest of the disciples, had expected Jesus to return in power during their lifetimes. As they began to die off the faith of many began to grow cold with doubt. It was necessary to re-new the authority of God in how His Kingdom was to be established.

So, how does this work? When one is ordained, confirmed to be under the authority of God, the elders of the church lay hands upon the head of the initi-ate to signify they have now come under the authority of God. Whatever happens is God's responsibility for whatever reason God may have. In other words, God is stating, "Suck it up Buttercup! Whatever you are fac-ing is part of My greater plan." A good example of that is provided in the Biblical story of Job wherein God advises a bitter Job to study the workings of the universe and try to explain it.

Now it may well be God's option to physically heal. But if He chooses not to do so at this time is not an indication of low faith. Ultimately the full healing for all involved will come at the final resurrection. At this time, like Job, the minds of those hanging by a wing and a prayer were troubled that the promised return of the Messiah was running so late. Like the members of my congregation, they needed reassurance that

God was still in charge. So, if it's actually regarding a physical issue, request an anointing but seek medical treatment as well.

Another translation issue deals with the old saying, "spare the rod and spoil the child. That apparent permission to beat our children was my first excursion into Bible research. As a youth it truly hit home with me. That my parents used it as the excuse to blister my butt or out and out clobber me as I grew too old to spank, while refusing to join me as I attended church on my own, prompted me to question the practice. While I inherently knew it was wrong, it would be decades before I discovered the truth of it was in the translation of the word used for rod.

This first scripture provides us with a clue in its wording regarding the withholding of discipline, but it still seems to encourage using a rod on him. I find it interesting how nowhere in these admonitions is a daughter threatened with such a beating. However, the rod in question derives from the original word **che-vet**. That was not a simple rod but the classic shepherd's hook curved staff. The rod portion was used in directing the sheep while the curved end was useful in pulling sheep out of whatever trouble they might have gotten themselves into. No shepherd ever beat his sheep. They were not laying down beside the still waters because they'd been beaten unconscious. "Thy rod (chevet) and thy staff, they **comfort** me." That chevet was a symbol of protection.

> Proverbs 23:13-14 Do not withhold discipline from a child; if you strike him with a rod, he will not die. If you strike him with the rod, you will save his soul from Sheol (the grave).

In the case Proverbs 14:24 the text is more accurately translated as follows: 'He who withholds proper direction exhibits lack of love towards his son.'

> Proverbs 14;24 Whoever spares the rod hates his son, but he who loves him is diligent to discipline him.

The remaining proverbs emphasize the point that this is about proper instruction and guidance not physical abuse though there might, on occasion, be a need to emphasize a point with a measured potch on the butt.

Proverbs 29:15 The rod and reproof give wisdom, but a child left to himself brings shame to his mother.

Proverbs 22:6 Train up a child in the way he should go; when he is old, he will not depart from it.

Way back when I delivered this alternative to the troubling concept of beating our children with a rod, the congregation erupted with applause. That was not the result of great oratory but relief at being freed from a hateful practice. So much else of what we have been falsely taught is in error. A study of the parables of Jesus will open our eyes even further.

However, before moving on, here follows the promised explanation of the three days and three nights between Good Friday sunset and Easter Sunday morning:

Now, this is no small matter. Jesus was approached by the Jewish religious leaders requesting a sign from Him. Jesus proclaimed the sign of Jonah to be the ONLY sign He would provide:

Matt12:38 Then some of the Pharisees and teachers of the law said to him, "Teacher, we want to see a sign from you."

³⁹ He answered, "A wicked and adulterous generation asks for a sign! But none will be given it except the sign of the prophet Jonah. 40 For as Jonah was three days and three nights in the belly of a huge fish, so the Son of Man will be three days and three nights in the heart of the earth. 41 The men of Nineveh will stand up at the judgment with this generation and condemn it; for they repented at the preaching of Jonah, and now something greater than Jonah is here.

What is the correct way to justify the "three days and three nights" promised in Matthew 12:40 ? Even should the apologist's explanation of a partial day being the same as a complete one, the explanation would not fit because in Jewish parlance each new day begins and ends at sunset. Jesus was laid in His tomb as the sun set meaning Friday was over. It would not have counted for even a partial day. The night and following Saturday day counted as one. The next sunset would have begun the second night. But the grave was already empty when the two women arrived at sunrise Sunday morning to anoint His body. There is absolutely no way in that scenario to fulfill the proof Jesus gave.

Since Jesus meant three literal days and three literal nights—72 full hours, if Jesus were in the tomb only from late Friday afternoon to sometime early Sunday morning, then the sign He gave that He was the prophesied Messiah was not fulfilled. What is the answer?

Behold, there is an obvious answer once you understand that this was during the Jewish Passover. This year, 2023, Pesach was observed on the same days as the year Jesus was crucified. The entire festival is held for 7 to 8 days in which no leavened products are to be consumed. The first and last days are considered to be High Sabbaths during which, as during the weekly Sabbath, no menial work is to be done. So, this year, as in the year Jesus suffered, Thursday was a high annual Sabbath Day observed in addition to the regular weekly Sabbath Day of Saturday.

Jesus held the Last Supper gathering Tuesday after which He went out to pray at the Garden of Gethsemane. There he was arrested and taken before Pilate. On Wednesday He was crucified, but the sacred rules forbade Him being left on the cross during the High Sabbath, so he was finished off and laid in the tomb as the sun set to begin the Thursday High Sabbath.

Mark 16:1 <u>When the Sabbath was over, the two Mary's</u> **bought spices** so they might come and anoint His body. Then, very early on the first day of the week, as the sun began to rise, they came to the tomb to discover the stone had previously been rolled away and Jesus was **<u>already risen</u>**.

Luke 24:1 Now upon the first day of the week, very early in the morning, they came unto the sepulchre, bringing the spices which they had pre-pared, and certain others with them. ² And they found the stone rolled away from the sepulchre. ³And they entered in and found not the body of the Lord Jesus. ⁴ And it came to pass, as they were much perplexed thereabout, behold, two men stood by them in shining garments: ⁵ And as they were afraid, and bowed down their faces to the earth, they said unto them, "Why seek ye the liv-ing among the dead? ⁶ He is not here but is risen: remember how he spake unto you when he was yet in Galilee?"

Note here how in Mark's account they went out AFTER THE SABBATH to purchase spices with which to anoint Jesus' body; but, in Luke's account they come VERY EARLY ON SUNDAY bringing the ointments which they HAD ALREADY PREPARED.

Wednesday: Jesus crucified

Sunset: Jesus laid in tomb – High Sabbath begins - one night

Thursday: High Sabbath - one day

Sunset: High Sabbath ends – two nights

Friday: Women purchase spices & prepare ointment - two days

Sunset: Weekly Sabbath begins – two nights

Saturday: Weekly Sabbath – three days

Sunset: Sabbath ends – three nights – Jesus leaves the tomb

Sunday: Women arrive at daybreak to find Him already off seeking coffee.

There you have it. How is it such learned theologians don't even GET that?!

AND SO MUCH ELSE

CHAPTER THIRTEEN

THE PARABLES

Merriam-Webster defines a parable as "a usually short fictitious story that illustrates a moral attitude or a religious principle." So, a parable was designed as a metaphorical tool Jesus used to conceal a truth He was attempting to privately get across to His disciples.

> Matt 13:10-13 And the disciples came and said to Him, "Why do You speak to them in parables?" He answered and said unto them," Because it is given unto you to know the mysteries of the kingdom of heaven, but to them it is not given. Therefore, speak I to them in parables: because they are

seeing see not; and hearing they hear not, neither do they understand."

Even so, Jesus still had to explain the inherent meaning to His followers. These next few examples illustrate the deeper meaning regarding God's ultimate intentions. So, then, know that the time has come for you to understand as well.

In the Parable of *The Good Samaritan*, the common focus is on doing virtuous deeds to strangers, but there is an even deeper meaning to the narrative. The story revolves around a Jewish traveler who is set upon by thieves who, beat, rob, and leave him for dead along the road. Many of his own, including a priest and a Pharisee, with the two religious leaders literally crossing to the opposite side of the road to avoid getting too close to someone considered to be unclean. At last, a Samaritan takes mercy on him, tending to his wounds and transporting him to an inn, where he pays the innkeeper to care for the unfortunate victim.

This all plays out as a simple story of compassion until a closer focus is directed upon the participants. The Samaritans were descended from surrounding gentile tribes who had been moved into Israel to replace the original Jewish inhabitants after they had been carried off into captivity by the conquering Babylonians. When the Jews returned to the Promised Land, they found it populated by the Samaritans. As a result, the two competing cultures got a 'mad on' towards each other. The ultimate lesson here has to do with the view of Jesus towards "who is my neighbor?"

> [25] On one occasion an expert in the law stood up to test Jesus. "Teacher," he asked, "what must I do to inherit eternal life?"[26] "What is written in the Law?" he replied. "How do you read it?"[27] He answered, "'Love the Lord your God with all your heart and with all your soul and with all your strength and with all your mind'[c]; and, 'Love your neighbor as yourself.'[d]"[28] "You have answered correctly," Jesus replied. "Do this and you will live."[29] But he wanted to justify himself, so he asked Jesus, "And who is my neighbor?"[30] In explanation Jesus related the Parable of the Good Samaritan...

In the next example, the Parable of **The Prodigal Son**, we learn of two brothers who go their separate ways. The elder brother stays home to manage the family business while the younger requested his inheritance and departs from his father's house to seek a life of depravity. However, after experiencing the harsh realities of life, the prodigal son realizes he should return to his father's home if only as a servant. In the immediate context, the prodigal son represented the tax collectors and sinners with whom Jesus associated. In modern terms, the prodigal son represents all sinners who squander and reject the blessings offered by God.

> *Luke 15:17–20* And when he came to himself, he said, how many hired servants of my father's house have bread enough and to spare, and I perish with hunger! I will arise and return to my father, and will say unto him, Father, I have sinned against heaven, and before thee, and am no longer worthy to be called thy son: make me as one of thy hired servants. And he arose and came to his father. But when he was yet a great way off, his father saw him, and had compassion, and ran, and fell on his neck, and kissed him. This implies the father was watching hopefully for the son's return.

In joy over the return of his lost son, the father hosts a celebration for which the fatted calf is BBQed. Not surprisingly, the faithful older brother was pissed off.

"Now his older son was in the field. And as he came and drew near to the house, he heard music and dancing. So, he called one of the servants and asked what these things meant.

"And he said to him, 'Your brother has come, and because he has received him safe and sound, your father has killed the fatted calf.'

"But he was angry and would not go in. Therefore, his father came out and pleaded with him. So, he answered and said to his father, 'Lo, these many years I have been serving you; I never transgressed your commandment at any time; and yet you never gave me a young goat,

The refusal of the older son to join the party directly relates to the refusal of Jesus' hearers to join him in partying with the sinners who had come to him. Likewise, we don't know if the older son ever joined the party. Oddly, this reflects how, even after receiving the vision in which the Apostle Peter was instructed to no longer consider unclean what the Lord has cleansed, he withdrew from eating with Gentiles when the legalistic Jerusalem delegation arrived. Do they ever come to accept sinners as he does? More importantly, do they ever come to accept heaven's joy at the repentance of sinners?

Here may, yet, be a further example of the older son's reaction when, at the final resurrection all the rest of the dead, who had gone the way of the prodigal son and died in their sins, are raised up and given their first real opportunity to apply Jesus the Christ in their lives. A further example of this is represented by the next two parables.

In Matt 18:23-31, Jesus is asked by Peter, "How many times am I required to forgive a brother who sins against me, seven times?"

No,"" Jesus answered, "seventy times seven!"

Obviously, this isn't limited to 4900 times; it means as often as necessary. In parallel with this, the Parable of the Workers in the Field expresses a clue as to how unlimited the Grace of God must be.

The parable of the Workers in the Field

Matt. 20:1-16 "For the kingdom of heaven is like a landowner who went early in the morning to hire workers for his vineyard. [2] He agreed to pay them a denarius[a] for the day and sent them into his vineyard.

[3] "About nine in the morning he went out and saw others standing in the marketplace doing nothing. [4] He told them, 'You also go and work in my vineyard, and I will pay you whatever is right.' [5] So they went.

"He went out again about noon and about three in the afternoon and did the same thing. [6] About five in the afternoon he went out and found still others standing around. He asked them, 'Why have you been standing here all day long doing nothing?'

[7] 'Because no one has hired us,' they answered.

"He said to them, 'You also go and work in my vineyard.'

"When evening came, the owner of the vineyard said to his foreman, 'Call the workers and pay them their wages, beginning with the last ones hired and going on to the first.'

[9] The workers who were hired about five in the afternoon came and each received a denarius. [10] So when those came who were hired first, they expected to receive more. But each one of them also received a denarius. [11] When they received it, they began to grumble against the landowner. [12] 'These

who were hired last worked only one hour,' they said, 'and you have made them equal to us who have borne the burden of the work and the heat of the day.'

[13] "But he answered one of them, 'I am not being unfair to you, friend. Didn't you agree to work for a denarius? [14] Take your pay and go. I want to give the one who was hired last the same as I gave you. [15] Don't I have the right to do what I want with my own money? Or are you envious because I am generous?'

[16] "So the last will be first, and the first will be last."

A hint into how he Gospel was to go out to all the world from Israel and be preached to the Gentiles is woven into this final example:

The parable of the Wedding

And Jesus answered and spoke unto them again by parables, and said, [2] The kingdom of heaven is like unto a certain king, which made a marriage for his son, [3] And sent forth his servants to call them that were bidden to the wedding: and they would not come. ⁴ Again, he sent forth other servants, saying, "tell them which are bidden, Behold, I have prepared my dinner: my oxen and my fatlings are killed, and all things are ready: come unto the marriage." ⁵ But they made light of it, and went their ways, one to his farm, another to his merchandise: ⁶ And the remnant took his servants, and treated them spitefully, and slew them.

⁷ But when the king heard thereof, he was wroth: and he sent forth his armies, and destroyed those murderers, and burned up their city. ⁸ Then saith he to his servants, "The wedding is ready, but they which had been bidden were not worthy.⁹ Go ye therefore into the highways, and as many as ye shall find, bid to the marriage.

¹⁰ So those servants went out onto the highways, and gathered together all as many as they found, both bad and good: and the wedding was furnished with guests. ¹¹ And when the king came in to see the guests, he saw there a man which had not on a wedding garment: ¹² And he saith unto him, "Friend, how camest thou in hither not having a wedding garment?" And he was speechless.¹³ Then said the king to the servants, "Bind him hand

and foot, and take him away, and cast him into outer darkness." There shall be weeping and gnashing of teeth.

[14] For many are called, but few are chosen.

This parable is basically about the universality of God's calling. In the beginning the disciples of Jesus thought of themselves as a private Jewish club. Until Peter experienced his epiphany, new converts were even required to be circumcised. By this Jesus teaches the Kingdom of God is open to everyone, not only Jews. This parable teaches God invites anyone willing to put on His Son. The parable teaches that God invites those willing to accept anyone willing to "put on" His son but ultimately rejecting any who attempt to enter based upon their own self-righteousness instead of His Grace.

In conclusion, we see how God's Grace is now portrayed as universal, how He is willing to forgive to the Nth degree and embrace the eventual return of all His 'lost sheep,' and unimpressed by the 'righteousness' of the religious leaders of His day. How do you think He feels about those weaving His Words today to suit their selfish goals?

In chapter 14 we shall explore how badly God has been represented **by His 'followers.'**

CHAPTER FOURTEEN

HERETICS AND HEROES

- Unless I am convicted by Scripture and plain reason-I do not accept the authority of popes …Martin Luther

History has presented us with a veritable rogue's gallery of religious 'leaders.' As has been quoted many times, "Lord, deliver us from evil… as well as those declaring, in your name, to stamp it out.

For the first few hundred years A.D. the church at Rome enjoyed limited monopoly over only Christian issues. After 380 A.D. Emperor Theodosius issued the

Edict of Thessalonica recognizing the catholic orthodoxy of Nicene Christians as the state religion of the
Roman Empire. From that point until Martin Luther,
an Augustinian priest, posted his 95 Theses to the
Wittenberg church door, it had been a steady slide into
the very depravity Jesus had warned about.(Matt. 16:6)

> Matt 16 "Beware the leaven of the Pharisees.
> And Sadducees."
>
> Matt 24: 5 "Many will come in my Name de-
> claring that I am the Christ and by so doing will
> deceive many."
>
> Mark 13;22 "If it were possible, even God's
> chosen ones would be deceived."

How did this occur? How is it the individual, yet
interdependent, house congregations formed by Paul
and the other evangelists of Jesus developed into
the very beast Jesus had warned of? Obviously, the
Deceiver had been very busy during the 'time' and
'times' of the Great Tribulation spread over the ensuing three century period. Rev 12;12-20.

Matters finally came to a head under the misrule
of **Pope Leo X** who was infamous for his statement,
"This fable has been most profitable for us." Can you

imagine such a statement being made by the purported head of the church? Along with the 'sale' of sinful indulgences, it is no wonder a Catholic monk, Martin Luther, was motivated to seek a reformation of his church.

> Indulgences hold a controversial place in the history of the Catholic Church. The buying and selling of indulgences is what helped to launch the Reformation. Indulgences began in about the ninth century A.D. as a means to bribe their way out of performing a set of tasks to fulfill penance for sins.

Luther's Most Influential Act

Luther could not have imagined in 1517 that his most influential act during the German Reformation, the act which would touch most lives and effect the budding Protestant movement the most would not be his Galatians or Romans commentaries, his theological tracts like "The Bondage of the Will," or even his insistence on justification by grace through faith alone. No, the biggest real waves in the ecclesiastical pool were produced by his production of the Lutheran Bible. Both Luther and William Tyndale deserve equal billing as the real pioneers of Bible translations from the original languages into that of ordinary people, "so they might read it, study it, learn it, and be moved and shaped by it." The Bible of the people, by the people, and especially for the people did not really exist before Luther and Tyndale.

Apparent agreement over the translation used did not, as history illustrates, further translate into uniformity of doctrine, however. Christian churches have been much like Chicago taverns with one on practically every block. Today there are more than 4500 separate denominations in the world: 200 or more just in the United States! How can this be if the Bible is considered the literal inerrant word of God? Well, as has been pointed out, scripture is more like a form of poetic imagery subject to individual interpretation than a hard set of rules.

Why you might ask, would God allow such confusion regarding His ministry? Why indeed can be asked right along with why does God allow evil in the first place? Why do the innocent suffer while evil seems to succeed? Ok, let's circle back to that forbidden tree of the Knowledge of Good and Evil. As much of a set-up as it seems to have been, God DID allow us the freedom to choose. And therein dwells the reason there is so much disagreement over what God wants from us, even though the true answer should be simple to parse out.

If we look within ourselves, we can see the truth of the matter that, whether collectively or individually, we are still trying to twist God's Word to suit our perceived narrative. Even the 1st Century church was struggling over this. In his first Epistle to the church at Corinth, the Apostle Paul called them out on their divisions of faith.

> 1 Cor. 1:10-12: I appeal to you, brothers and sisters,[a] in the name of our Lord Jesus Christ, that all of you agree with one another in what you say and that there be no divisions among you, but that you be perfectly united in mind and thought. 11 My brothers and sisters, some from Chloe's household have informed me that there are quarrels among you. 12 What I mean is this: One of you says, "I follow Paul"; another, "I follow Apollos"; another, "I follow Cephas[b]"; still another, "I follow Christ." 2 And so it was with me, brothers and sisters. When I came to you, I did not come with eloquence or human wisdom as I proclaimed to you the testimony about God.[a] 2 For I resolved to know nothing while I was with you except Jesus Christ and him

crucified. [3] I came to you in weakness with great fear and trembling. [4] My message and my preaching were not with wise and persuasive words, but with a demonstration of the Spirit's power, [5] so that your faith might not rest on human wisdom, but on God's power.

God's Wisdom Revealed by the Spirit

[6] We do, however, speak a message of wisdom among the mature, but not the wisdom of this age or of the rulers of this age, who are coming to nothing. [7] No, we declare God's wisdom, a mystery that has been hidden and that God destined for our glory before time began. [8] None of the rulers of this age understood it, for if they had, they would not have crucified the Lord of glory. [9] However, as it is written:

"What no eye has seen,
    what no ear has heard,
and what no human mind has conceived"[b]—
    the things God has prepared for those who love him—
[10] these are the things God has revealed to us by his Spirit.

There were intense disputes between Paul, Peter, James, and the various other evangelists with ties to Jerusalem over whether salvation was by Works, Grace, or a complex formula. They even fought over whether the message of Jesus was a private Jewish message which only the circumcised were permitted to take part in. Many remained convinced the Messiah would soon return to supplant the Roman Empire with a restoration of the Kingdom of Israel. And that was within a lifetime of when Jesus walked the earth.

Just imagine how many doctrinal variations could be worked up since then! That is why, I believe, God has allowed us so much time and opportunity to try out every other option including non-Christian theology. Humanity is collectively compiling a history from which we will, at the end of days, be instructed when "the 'books' are opened," (Rev. 20:12) and the rest of the dead are 'judged' (administered) from what (our entire human history) is written therein.

Consider the massive religious dumpster fire that has spread from out of the Protestant Reformation ignited by Martin Luther. represented by the differences between the Lutheran and Calvinist doctrines. The basis for all the disparate theologies observed today was formed long before in the middle 5th century.

Augustine of Hippo, who lived from 354 to 430 A.D. is commonly considered to be the Father of Modern Religious Thought. He certainly was far ahead of his time when it comes to speculating on the nature of God and the creation of all things including time itself. He even suggested the Genesis creation account was only allegorical. Tis a shame he was so messed up when it came to sexuality. Maybe ,even more so, it's a shame he never mastered Greek. It would cost him dearly.

The next chapter will explore this theologian often referred to as The Father of Western Theological Thought; but first, in honor of free thinkers everywhere, here follow some of my favorite heretics:

Origenes Adamantius of Alexandria:, born about 185, was the first theologian to formulate a systematic system.. Believed to have been educated by his father, Leonidas, he used this education to revive and teach, as didascalies, at the "catechetical school in Alexandria in 203, under Bishop Demetrius. This was after his father died as a martyr in 202 CE in the persecutions under Roman Emperor Septimius Severus. Origen was then seventeen and apparently succeeded Clement of Alexandria who had been driven out of town by the persecutions. He lived in a turbulent period for the Christian Church, a period of Roman persecutions and loose doctrinal consensus. He was ordained as a priest under controversial conditions. His writings were extensive, much of which has been lost. In later centuries some extreme views by followers were attributed to him and his name was brought under suspicion of heresy denying him a official rank of sainthood. He was anathemized by the 2nd Council of Constantinople in 553, specifically in its eleventh Canon:

In around 215 he went to Palestine where he was invited to preach by Alexander, bishop of Jerusalem, and Theocritus, bishop of Caesarea, even though he was not ordained. His teaching there was considered a breach of discipline by Demetrius.

In 230, he was ordained a priest in Palestine by Bishops Alexander and Theocritus. His views on the nature of time, God, and universal salvation were well ahead of his time – or, perhaps, fading remnants of the true Gospel. Such expression lacked the authority of Demetrius who subsequently expelled him from Alexandria. Following his expulsion, he founded a school in Caesarea. He died a martyr's death in the persecutions of 250, probably in 254, and most probably in Caesarea.

Manichaeism: is a former major universal offshoot founded in the 3rd century AD by the Parthian prophet Mani. Manichaeism teaches an elaborate dualistic cosmology describing the struggle between a good spiritual world of light and an evil material World of Darkness. Through an ongoing process that takes place in human history, life is gradually removed from the world of matter and returned to the world of light, from whence it came. Mani's teaching was intended to combine, succeed, and surpass the teachings of Christianity and Zoroastrianism.

Pelagius: c. 354–418 was a theologian known for promoting a system of doctrines (termed Pelagianism by his opponents) which emphasized human choice in salvation and denied original sin. Pelagius was accused of heresy at the synod of Jerusalem in 415. His doctrines were harshly criticized by St. Augustine, especially the Pelagian views about mankind's good inner nature and individual responsibility for choosing ascetism. Pelagius especially stressed the freedom of human will. Very little is known about the personal life and career of Pelagius.

Galileo Galilee: Born in 1654, this guy is likely my favorite heretic, not just for his inquisitive mind but also, for his literary style of lampooning the Pope and those others too blinded by orthodoxy to even consider evidence contrary to what were instructed to believe. Einstein referred to him as Father of the Scientific Method.

Galileo's technical adjustments to the telescope made it possible to bring into focus the proof of the Copernican hypothesis of the sun being the center of a heliocentric solar system in which the earth was no longer viewed as the center point of the universe. As is still the case with some today, at that the time all scripture was officially declared to be the literal inspired words of God. His proofs contradicted such scriptures as I Chron 16:30 "The world is established that it cannot be moved", Eccl. 1:5 "The Sun also arises and then goes down and hastens to the place from where he arose," Ps. 104:19-21 "God appointed the Moon for seasons; and the Sun know his going down." Other such scriptures include Ps. 104:5, Ps. 96:10, Ps. 93:1. Heaven was believed to be in the clouds and Hell at the opposite extreme in the center of the earth. There are still self-delusional folks who believe scripture over reslity.

If Galileo was correct in his assertions, then scripture must be in error. For this he was accused of heresy, but it was his lampooning of Pope Urban as the character of **Simplicio** in his 1632 work, *Dialogues on Two Sciences* which really got him condemned into trouble. Urvan had been a good friend and supporter. Insulting his intelligence was more than the Pope could endure, although he still protected Galileo from the ultimate fate of a heretic. So, while his sentence of life imprisonment under house arrest wasn't the result Galileo had hoped for, it was better than what his contemporary, Giordano Bruno suffered.

Giordano Bruno Italian: C 1548 – 17 February 1600) An Italian philosopher, poet, and cosmological theorist chiefly focused on the relationship between human beings, the cosmos, and God. Many of them, like the teachings of The Way of Christ, were moral exhortations calling for a way of life leading to spiritual rebirth, and eventually to divinization] He is known for his cosmological theories, which conceptually extended to include the then novel Copernican hypothesis that the stars were distant suns surrounded by their own planets, and he raised the possibility that these planets might foster life of their own. He also insisted that the universe, like God, is infinite.

The Inquisition found him guilty of heresy on several issues, and he was burned at the stake in 1600 after first having his tongue nailed to the roof of his mouth to shut him up. Ahhh, Churchianity!!! After his death, he gained considerable fame, being particularly celebrated by 19th- and early 20th-century commentators who regarded him as a martyr for science. Although most historians believe his heresy trial was not in response to his cosmological views but rather a due to his religious views, many still contend that the main reason was indeed his cosmological views which disturbed the divine order of the church. Likely it was from all things considered. Bruno's case is still considered a landmark in the history of free thought and the emerging sciences.

––––––––––––––––

William Tyndale c. 1494 – c. 6 October 1536) was an English biblical scholar and linguist who became a leading figure in the Protestant Reformation in the years leading up to his execution. He is well known for translating the Bible into common English and was influenced by the teachings of Martin Luther. Tyndale's translation was the first English Bible to draw directly from Hebrew and Greek texts, the first English translation to take advantage of the printing press, the first of the new English Bibles of the Reformation, and the first English translation to use "Jehovah" as God's name as preferred by English Protestant Reformers. It was taken to be a direct challenge to the hegemony of the Catholic Church and of those laws of England maintaining the church's position. The work of Tyndale continued to play a key role in spreading Reformation ideas across the English-speaking world and eventually across the British Empire.

Peter of Bruys (also known as **Pierre de Bruys or Peter de Bruis**; c 1117 – c.1131) was a medieval French religious teacher. He was called a heresiarch (leader of a heretical movement) by the Roman Catholic Church because he opposed infant baptism, the erecting of churches, the veneration of crosses, the doctrine of transubstantiation, and prayers for the dead. An angry Roman Catholic mob murdered him in or around CE 1131.

Peter Waldo: More than three hundred years before Martin Luther was born, an unlikely reformer suddenly appeared in the city of Lyon in southeast France. His protests against doctrines and practices of the Roman Catholic Church were strong tremors foretelling the coming spiritual earthquake called the Reformation. And the movement he launched indeed would survive to join the great Reformation. He is known in history as Peter Waldo.

Many details about Waldo are not known, including his name. We don't know if Peter was his real first name since it doesn't appear in any document until 150 years after his death. His last name was most likely something like *Valdés* — *Valdo* (Waldo) was the Italian adaptation. We also don't know the year Peter was born or the precise year he died — historians disagree over whether he died between 1205 and 1207 or between 1215 and 1218.

But we do know a few earthshaking things. A Rich Ruler Repents:

In 1170, Waldo was a very wealthy, well-known merchant in the city of Lyon. He had a wife, two daughters, and lots of property. But something happened — some say he witnessed the sudden death of a friend; others say he heard a spiritual song of a traveling minstrel — and Waldo became deeply troubled over the spiritual state of his soul and desperate to know how he could be saved.

The first thing he resolved was to read the Bible. But since it only existed in the Latin Vulgate, and his Latin was poor, he hired two scholars to translate it into the vernacular so he could study it.

Next, he sought spiritual counsel from a priest, who pointed out the example of the rich young ruler mentioned in the Gospels and quoted Jesus: "One thing you still lack. Sell all that you have and distribute to the poor, and you will have treasure in heaven; and come, follow me" (Luke 18:23a0. Jesus' words pierced Waldo's heart. Like the rich young ruler, Waldo suddenly realized he had been serving Mammon, not God. But unlike the rich young ruler who walked away from Jesus, Waldo repented, and did exactly what Jesus had advised: after making provision for his wife and daughters, he gave away all his stuff to the poor. From then on, he determined to live in complete dependence upon God for his provision.

Waldo began to preach from his Bible in the streets of Lyon, especially to the poor. Many were converted, and by 1175 a sizable group of men and women had become Waldo's disciples. They too gave away their possessions and were preaching (women as well as men). The people started calling them the "Poor of Lyons." Later, as the group grew into a movement and spread throughout France and other parts of Europe, they became known as "The Waldensians."

The more Waldo studied Scripture, the more troubled he became over certain doctrines, practices, and governing structures of the Catholic Church — not to mention its wealth. And he boldly spoke out against these things. But since the Church officially prohibited lay preaching, Waldo and his ragtag band drew opposition from church leaders.

The Archbishop of Lyons was particularly irked by this uneducated, self-appointed reform movement and moved to squash it. But in 1179, Waldo appealed directly to Pope Alexander III and received his approval. However, only five years later the new pope, Lucius III, sided with the archbishop and excommunicated Waldo and his followers.

In the earlier years, much like that of Martin Luther, the *Waldensian* heresy was a simply a reform movement. Waldo had never intended to leave the church, and he held onto numerous traditional Catholic doctrines. But after the excommunication, and continuing beyond Waldo's death, the Waldensian's Protestant-like convictions increased and solidified to include the following:

- They rejected all claims to authority besides Scripture.
- They rejected all mediators between God and man, except the Avatar of Jesus (though Mary was venerated for quite a while).
- They rejected the doctrine that only a priest could hear confession and argued that all believers were qualified.
- They rejected purgatory, and thus rejected indulgences and prayers for the dead.
- They believed the only Scripture-sanctioned sacraments were baptism and communion.
- They rejected the Church's emphasis on fast and feast days and eating restrictions.
- They rejected the priestly and monastic caste system.
- They rejected the veneration of relics, pilgrimages, and the use of holy water.
- They rejected the pope's claim to authority over earthly rulers.
- They eventually rejected the apostolic succession of the pope.

Cathars and the Albigensian Crusade or the **Cathar Crusade** (French: *Croisade des albigeois*; 1209–1229) was a military and ideological campaign initiated by Pope Innocent III to eliminate Catharism that pretty much represents the basic reason why we don't GET God even to this day.

The *Cathars* originated from an anti-materialist reform movement within the Bogomil churches of the Balkans calling for what they saw as a return to the Christian message of perfection, poverty and preaching, combined with a rejection of the lusts of the flesh. The reforms were a reaction against the often perceived scandalous and dissolute lifestyles of the Catholic clergy. Their theology, Gnostic in many ways, was basically dualistic. Several of their practices, especially their belief in the inherent evil of the physical world, conflicted with the doctrines of the Incarnation of Christ and Catholic Sacraments. This led to accusations of Gnosticism and attracted the ire of the Catholic establishment. They became known as the Albigensians because many were adherents from the city of Albi and the surrounding area in the 12th and 13th centuries.

Between 1022 and 1163, the Cathars were condemned by eight local church councils, the last of which, held at Tours, declared that all Albigenses should be put into prison and have their property confiscated. Pope Innocent III's diplomatic attempts to roll back Catharism were met with little success. After the murder of his legate in 1208, Innocent III declared a crusade against the Cathars. He offered the lands of the Cathar heretics to any French nobleman willing to take up arms.

From 1209 to 1215, the Crusaders experienced great success, capturing Cathar lands and systematically crushing the movement. From 1215 to 1225, a series of revolts caused many of the lands to be regained by the Cathars. A renewed crusade resulted in the recapturing of the territory and effectively drove *Catharism* underground by 1244. The *Albigensian Crusade* had a role in the creation and institutionalization of both the Dominican Order and the Medieval Inquisition. The Dominicans promulgated the message of the Church and spread it by preaching the Church's teachings in towns and villages to stop the spread of alleged heresies, while the Inquisition investigated people who were accused of supporting heresies. Because of these efforts, all discernible traces of the Cathar movement were eradicated by the middle of the 14th century.

Some historians consider the Albigensian Crusade against the Cathars an act of genocide.

The word "Cathar" is derived from the Greek word *katharos*, meaning "clean" or "pure." As such, Cathars rejected the Catholic Priesthood, labelling its members, including the pope, unworthy and corrupted. Disagreeing on the Catholic concept of the unique role of the priesthood, they taught that anyone, not just the priest, could consecrate the Eucharistic host or hear a confession. There were, however, men selected amongst the Cathars to serve as bishops and deacons. *Cathars* rejected the dogma of the physical presence of Christ in the Eucharist and Catholic teaching on the existence of Purgatory.

The *Cathars* were part of a widespread spiritual reform movement in medieval Europe which began about CE 653 when Constantine Silvanus brought a copy of the Gospels to Armenia. In the following centuries a number of dissenting groups arose, gathered around charismatic preachers, who rejected the authority of the Catholic Church. These groups based their beliefs and practices on the Gospels rather than on Church dogma and sought a return to the original message of the apostles. Sects such as the Paulicians in Armenia, Bogomils from Bulgaria and the Balkans, Arnoldists in Northern Italy, Petrobrucians, in the South of France, Henricians in Switzerland and France, and Waldensians of the Piedmont area on the border of France and Italy, were violently persecuted and repressed. The Paulicians were burned to death as heretics; the Bogomils were expelled from Serbia and subjected to the Inquisition and the Bosnian Crusade; Peter de Bruys, leader of the Petrobrucians, was pushed into a bonfire by an angry mob in 1131.

A number of prominent 12th century preachers insisted on it being the responsibility of the individual to develop a relationship with God, independent of an established clergy. Henry of Lausanne criticized the priesthood and called for lay reform of the Church. He gained a large following.[Henry's preaching focused on condemning clerical corruption and clerical hierarchy, and there is no evidence that he subscribed to Cathar teachings on dualism.[He was arrested around 1146 and never heard from again. Arnold of Brescia, leader of the Arnoldists, was hanged in 1155 and his body burnt and thrown into the Tiber River "for fear", one chronicler says, "lest the people might collect them and honor them as the ashes of a martyr."

The Waldensians, followers of Peter Waldo, experienced burnings and massacres.

In 1209, Pope Innocent III decided to crack down on heretics like the Cathars. That the Catholics and Cathars of Beziers had lived there together for many years in relative harmony apparently didn't much matter to the Vatican. On July 22, 1209, as they were celebrating the annual Feast of Mary Magdalene together, a religious holiday observed by various Christian religions, an army of "Crusaders" sent by Pope Innocent III showed up outside the walls of the town.

The military leader of the army was Simon de Montfort, a French nobleman highly motivated by the Pope's promise that he could keep the land of any heretics he killed. The Crusaders were accompanied by an official representative of the Pope, a French Cistercian monk named Arnaud Amalric. When the leaders of Beziers refused to turn over the town's Cathar heretics to him the Crusaders attacked.

According to accounts written decades later, as the attack began, a soldier asked Amalric how they would be able to tell which Beziers townspeople were Catholics and which were Cathars. Amalric supposedly answered,

"Caedite eos. Novit enim Dominus qui snt eius."

("Kill them all. God will recognize his own.")

Martin Luther: 10 November 1483 – 18 February 1546) The Catholic dam holding back the free flow of Spiritual independence was finally breached by this German priest, theologian, author, hymnwriter, professor, and Augustinian Friar. He was the seminal figure of the Protestant Reformation, and his theological beliefs form the basis of Lutheranism.

Luther was ordained to the priesthood in 1507. He came to reject several teachings and practices of the Roman Catholic Church. In particular, he disputed the view on indulgences (basically bribery for sin). Luther proposed an academic discussion of the practice and efficacy of indulgences in his *Ninety-five theses* of 1517. His refusal to renounce all of his writings at the demand of Pope Leo X in 1520 and the Holy Roman Emperor Charles V at the Diet of Worms in 1521 resulted in his excommunication and condemnation as an outlaw by the emperor. Luther died in 1546 with Pope Leo X's excommunication still in effect.

Luther taught salvation and, consequently, eternal life are not earned by good deeds; rather, they are received only as the free gift of God's grace through the believer's faith in Jesus Christ, the redeemer from sin. His theology challenged the authority and office of the pope by teaching that the Bible is the only source of divinely revealed knowledge and opposed sacerdotalism by considering all baptized Christians to be a holy priesthood. Those who identify with these, and all of Luther's wider teachings, are called Lutherans, though Luther insisted on *Christian* or *Evangelical evangelisch* as the only acceptable names for individuals who professed Christ.

His translation into German vernacular instead of Latin made it more accessible to the laity, an event that had a tremendous impact on both the church and German culture. It fostered the development of a standard version of the German language added several principles to the art of translation and influenced the writing of an English translation by William Tyndale. His hymns influence the development of singing in Protestant churches. His marriage to Katarina Von Bora, a former set a model for the practice of clerical marriage amongst the Protestant clergy.

_____

William Tyndale: Despite originally being authorized by King James to produce an English language version of the Bible, Rome saw to it that he would pay the price for his heresy of making it possible for us to have a copy in every motel room.

Tyndale's translation of the Bible was used for subsequent English translations. One estimate suggests that the New Testament in the King James Version is 83% Tyndale's words and the Old Testament 76%.

In 1530, Tyndale wrote *The Practice of Prelates*, opposing King Henry VIII's plan to seek the annulment of his marriage on the grounds it as against scripture.

As a result of angering the King, Tyndale sought refuge in the Flemish territory of the Catholic Charles V. What could he have been thinking? In 1535 Tyndale was arrested and jailed for over a year. In 1536 he was convicted of heresy for his sin of translating the Bible into common English and executed by strangulation, after which his body was burnt at the stake. What a perfect representation of the lengths to which the corporate church will go to maintain power... even after their sacred cow had escaped the barn.

In 2002, Tyndale was placed 26th in the BBC's poll of the 100 greatest Brits.

So, when the ever-sanctimonious mob wonders why I so proudly wave the flag of heresy, looking back at this incomplete list of heroes of "The Way," I can only laugh and hope I'm living up to such a high standard.

CHAPTER FIFTEEN

ST· AUGUSTINE

Augustine of Hippo, who lived from 354 to 430 A.D. is commonly considered to be the *Father of Modern Christian Thought*. He certainly was far ahead of his time when it came to speculating on the nature of God and the creation of all things including time itself. How he came to his understanding is a story worth telling.

Aurelius Augustinas was a young man like most others of his time. He was born of Berber parentage from the Algerian quarter of north Africa. His mother was of Christian beliefs and ran her household in the Roman style of the day. Her headstrong son, however, rebelled against just about any attempt to control his carnal appetites. His original religious bent was toward the Manichean teachings which emphasized the earthly rule of a malevolent god in opposition to the heavenly rule of a merciful one. Although social pressure eventually motivated him to deny that belief, I contend it colored his ultimate perspective on grace.

Although enrolled in highly regarded schools where he excelled in rhetoric, he rebelled against his Greek instructions due to the physical brutality of his instructor. Once again, his basic willfulness caused him regrets later in life when his weakness in that far more expressive language would affect his understanding of God's deeper points. Latin, in which he excelled, was incapable of properly defining the deeper poetic moments of scripture, He, nevertheless became a powerful orator and established a school where he taught rhetoric. While teaching at the royal court of Milan he met with St. Ambrose who prompted him to re-evaluate Christian teachings. Then one day he overheard a child's voice say, "Take up and read."

Paul's epistle to the Romans was at hand, and from it he read *"Not in rioting and drunkenness, not in chambering and wantonness, not in strife and envying, but put on the Lord Jesus Christ, and make no provision for the flesh to fulfill the lusts thereof."* The rest would be destined to grow like the proverbial mustard seed. Following his baptism in 387

Augustine would turn away from teaching rhetoric to focus on preaching and studying the deeper issues of Christianity. By 395 he was ordained as Bishop of Hippo and preached several thousand sermons.

Augustine had been far from what we might consider saint-like. As a youth he had given in to his hormonal impulses, taking up with a girl of lower social status who bore him a son. After his family did the usual thing and arranged a "proper marriage" for their son, he was "forced" to reject her and put her out of his life. I struggle to imagine how this traumatic event affected him having learned how deeply he "loved" her. He obviously had a truly hard struggle over his sexuality praying, "Lord, grant me abstinence, but not yet." After his conversion, he turned to a monastic life of preaching and interpreting scripture. Augustine finally decided sexual activity and true righteousness were mutually exclusive. The arranged marriage never came about.

WHY FOCUS UPON AUGUSTINE? Pretty much everything that was to come up with the future doctrinal issues, first through Martin Luther, John Calvin, John Wesley, the Baptists and all the other schisms, both good and bad, can be traced back to the polemics of St. Augustine.

Augustine's concept of Original Sin was an incredibly fatalistic view of humankind. He referred to humans as the 'condemned masses' because we are conceived in sin, and thus damned from the moment of conception. Baptism was required as the initiation ritual to wash away this Original Sin, but it did not eliminate the human proclivity for evil. As he knew, baptized Christians (like himself) continued to sin in both body and mind.

At this point I want to step in and contend with this true master of oratory. I really wish he and I could meet mano e' mano. This is the nexus where my concept of what we don't GET alters the future arc of Christian thought. He, correctly, saw that only the Grace of God could absolve Mankind from the wages of sin. He also struggled with why so many resisted what was so obviously a gift (Grk: *chairs*).Augustine, also, saw God as omnipotent, omniscient, and omnipresent. How then was it possible for humans to resist the irresistible?

His conclusion was the basis for Calvinism; *God must only be interested in saving those He had preordained to be His. The rest could, literally, go to Hell.* "Because God is omniscient (all-knowing), He already knows who will be saved and who will be damned." Those not predetermined to life were simply chaff for the fires of

Hell. This must have seemed inconceivable to him, but he could see no other answer. Have hope and hang in there with me, 'cause I have the answer he was blinded from seeing. But first let's deal with this ***Doctrine of Original Sin***!

According to Augustine, we are all tainted by original sin through birth. Conceived in sin and born of woman there is no such thing as an innocent baby. But wait! What about Jesus? Even if He was fathered by God rather than man, he was still born of woman. How was He not vaginally tainted?

Easy, as in the doctrine of the Immaculate Conception, the Catechism of the Catholic Church teaches that Mary was also without sin. As you can well imagine, I have several problems with this assumption. If Mary never sinned, how about when she and Jesus' brothers showed up at His first healing to take him under control and haul him away? Wasn't that showing she doubted Him? Beyond that. She showed up with Jesus' brothers. What? Where'd they come from? I thought she was a perpetual virgin.

Beyond that, if original sin resulted from the process of conception through birth, Mary's mother would have had to be sinless, too... and her grandmother and so on and so forth all the way back to Mother Eve, who was certainly not without sin. No, all this comes as a result of the trauma suffered by Augustine as a direct result of his inability to control both of his heads, Hey, welcome to the club.

Besides, we have no need for original sin. Augustine already knew evil arose from the human weakness of willpower in both physical and mental aspects: the desire to satisfy bodily instincts and the willful desire to disobey for its own sake (the way in which Augustine understood his youthful act of stealing his neighbor's pears). "Sin is the inability to resist temptation. Matter itself is not evil, but overindulgence in matter and one's attitude toward matter can be evil. Humans are held responsible for evil and will be judged by God. So, have no concern for all those unbaptized babies floating about in Purgatory.

So, you might wonder, did this guy get anything right? Sure, there are a number of issues he pondered. The biggest concepts that interest me deal with the nature of creation and what is real.

Augustine argued that God had created everything in the universe simultaneously and not over a period of six days. He argued the six-day structure of creation presented in the Book of Genesis represents a logical framework, rather than the passage of time in a physical way – it would bear a spiritual, rather than physical, meaning, which is no less literal. One reason for this is the Apocryphal phrase in Sirach 18:1 creavit omnia simul ("He created all things at once"), which Augustine took as proof that the days of Genesis 1: had to be taken non-literally. As an additional support for describing the six days of creation as a heuristic device (poetic moment). Augustine thought the actual event of creation would be incomprehensible by humans and therefore needed to be translated into something simplistic. Of course, the proper translation of Gen 1:2 clears up any confusion regarding time.

Speaking of time, Augustine showed tremendous insight into that subject, as well. Augustine's **Confessions** demonstrate his understanding of time and eternity. "Time," according to Augustine, "is the process by which our soul is 'stretched out' within the temporal so that we experience life events successively." Augustine finds, within time, the key to understanding our relationship with God is perceiving **The Eternal Awareness** exists solely outside of time. Hence, the meaninglessness of pondering what may have existed before God. Since time itself is part of the physical universe, it doesn't exist apart from it. There was no past with the "Being" simply known as "I Am."

Coming in an age before Dr. Who, that was quite a perceptive concept.

Aurelius Augustinus Hipponensis of Hippo was by far the greatest of the Christian Church Fathers. More than any other writer, he developed what would become known as systematic theology, or an explanation of how our faith fits into views of the universe, creation, and humankind's relationship with the unknowable. That he was imperfect matters little other than providing us the encouragement to grow in the faith as well. He also wavered on occasion, second guessing his assumptions. In one instance he declared Adam and Eve were originally created to be mortal; while he occasionally speculated their sin cost them immortality. Of course, proper punctuation could render that to be a simple matter of cause and effect.

His attitude towards the effect of hormones was, also, the reason for this alpha misogynist to declare the female sex was good for one thing only and should be afterwards shut away in sackcloth and ashes. "After all." He pondered, "If it was a companion Adam require, what would have been wrong with providing him with another man?"

When Martin Luther (1483-1546), a former Augustinian friar, protested against the Catholic

Church, he started the Protestant Reformation utilizing the teachings of Augustine. Through the various Protestant denominations and their missions, the Christian Western tradition is indebted to the teachings of Augustine. This shockwave eventually resulted in the Protestant Bible of 66 books in about 1825 when the British and Foreign Bible Society, in essence, threw down the gauntlet and said, "These 66 books and no others." Though there is still much to be gleaned from studying the Apocryphal scriptures.

Protestants had long treated these extra books as, at best, deuterocanonical. Some had even called them non-canonical, and there were some precedents for printing a Bible without these books. For example, there was a minority edition of the Great Bible from after 1549 that did not include the Apocrypha, and a 1575 edition of the Bishop's Bible also excluded those books. The 1599 and 1640 printings of the Geneva Bible left them out as well. But in any event, these books had not been treated as canonical by many Protestants. When the Luther Bible was produced based on Erasmus' work on the Greek New Testament, there were only a handful of Greek manuscripts Erasmus could consult, and they were not all that old. When the KJV was produced in 1611, there was the same problem both in regard to the Old Testament and the New Testament.

Today, to speak just of English, there are more than 900 translations or paraphrases of the New Testament in whole or in part into our language. Nine hundred! None of the original Reformers could have envisioned this nor for that matter could they have imagined so many common people having Bibles not just in the pulpits and pews but having their own Bibles in their own homes. The genie let out of the bottle at the beginning of the German Reformation turned out to be the Holy Spirit, "who makes all things new." Despite the raging of ecclesiastical tantrums such as the Spanish Inquisition, there was to be no return to the dark days of Tribulation.

But wait! The Tribulation was to be for a "time, times, and half a time." Despite the assertion of St. Augustine that the whole was representative of a single period of three and a half years, I assert the prophecy was for more than one period of time. I believe we still have that to-be-cut-short moment in time yet to come.

CHAPTER SIXTEEN

THE END GAME

At the end of his days, banished by Emperor Domitian to the Island of Patmos, the lone remaining physical companion of Jesus was making record of an apocalyptic host of visions. Most Christians avoid this final defining book of our Bible. Too many find the imagery disturbingly vague if not just outright disturbing. But I have recently come to see the Apocalypse as my favorite of all the Bible's contents. I am particularly fond of the final three chapters of St. John's Revelation as the key to understanding just what God has been up to all these ages. Understanding this is key to answering the questions of why God allows evil, why the innocent suffer while the wicked seem to prosper, and just what is the purpose of life?

Interested? Of course, you are. You wouldn't still be hanging around with me were you not. So, then, to begin, St. John was visited by an angel with instructions to write to seven congregations in Asia regarding what was to come to pass in the future. While he was commanded to send remonstrances and encouragements to those congregations, many believe the churches mentioned in the first three chapters represent characteristics of seven distinct eras through which the church would pass. The ensuing chapters deal with what would occur towards the end times under the rule of the Antichrist.

Then, at last, John records imagery most have fumbled, few have understood, and fewer still have picked up and run with. It is, to me, so earthshaking that I'm constantly in awe of the vision it provides. While most of the what, how, and why of the spiritual 'world' is still beyond human understanding, It totally illustrates what an awesome architect our God happens to be.

1. In the 20th chapter of his Apocalypse, John picks up the narrative, during the great battle called

Armageddon, at the point where Jesus returns and puts an end to the nonsense before it could result in the total annihilation (***tohu wa bohu***?) of all life on earth (Matt. 22-24). Back in the day, I would imagine such a concept would have been unimaginable; but today such a cataclysm is well within our perception. The fact John revealed that possibility is a further example of scripture being God breathed.

Rev. 20:1 shows who is to blame for the strife in our world:

I saw an angel coming down from heaven, having the key to the bottomless pit and a great chain in his hand.[8]He laid hold of the dragon, that serpent of old, who is the Devil and Satan, and bound him for a thousand years; and he cast him into the bottomless pit, and shut him up, and set a seal on him, so that he should deceive the nations no more till the thousand years were finished. But after these things he must be released for a little while.

Believers who have died 1 Thes. 4:13-17

[13] Brothers and sisters, we want you to know about those who sleep] so that you won't mourn like others who have no hope. [14] Since we believe that Jesus died and rose, so we also believe that God will bring with him those who have died in Jesus. [15] What we are saying is a message from the Lord: we who are alive and still around at the Lord's coming will not precede those who have died. [16] This is because the Lord himself will come down from heaven with the signal of a shout and a blast of God's trumpet. First, those who are dead in Christ will rise. [17] Then, we who are living and still around will be taken up together with them in the clouds to meet with the Lord in the air. And so shall we ever be with the Lord. [18] So encourage each other with these words.

Once the returned and glorified Christ has removed the influence of Satan, all those who had been "saved" and resurrected with those believers still alive at the advent, after meeting him in the clouds, will return with Him to establish and administer the Kingdom of God on earth. Without the interference of Satan, the Millennium will be a time of peace for all the remaining nations of earth.

And I saw thrones, and they sat on them, and judgment was committed to them. Then I saw the souls of those who had been beheaded for their witness to Jesus and for the word of God, who had not worshiped the beast or his image, and had not received his mark on their foreheads or on their hands. And they lived and reigned with Christ for a thousand years.

While it is not explicit who was seated on the thrones. "The natural construction is that the saints of God sat on them as administrators ruling over the newly established kingdom of Heaven on earth.

I saw thrones on which were seated those who had been given authority to judge ..."Thy kingdom come; thy will be done on earth aa it is in heaven.

American theologian Albert Barnes notes the "considerable resemblance, in many respects, between this [wording] and the statement in Daniel 7:9":

As I looked, thrones were set in place, and the Ancient of Days took his seat. The Ancient of Days came, and judgment was given for the saints of the Most High, and the time came when the saints possessed the kingdom.

and so the Cambridge Bible for Schools and Colleges argues that those seated on the thrones are these saints of the Most High.

Verse 5

But the rest of the dead lived not again until the thousand years were finished. This is the first resurrection.

Verse 6

Blessed and holy is he who has taken part in the first resurrection. Over such the second death has no power, but they shall be priests of God and of Christ and shall reign with Him a thousand years.

"Of God and of Christ": This provides a strong proof for the doctrine of Christ's coequal Deity with The Father.

Verse 10

Then the devil, who had deceived them, was thrown into the lake of fire, joining the beast and the false prophet. There they will be tormented day and night forever and ever.

Of course, since we're dealing with spirit beings, I doubt the fire matters beyond knowledge they are now fully cut off from God. Note, also, that the 'beast,' the false government of the anti-Christ, is consumed there-in. Other scriptures mention death and hades will be consumed there-in as well. Obviously, the Lake of Fire is allegorical in nature. Up to this point, most theologians are in general agreement as to the meaning of Revelation. It is in verse 12 that the narrative gets really interesting. So, as an airline pilot once advised as we prepared to launch from the short runway of Chicago's Midway Airport, "fasten your seatbelts, folks and hang on tight!"

Verse 12

And I saw the dead, small and great, standing before God, and books were opened. And another book was opened, which is the Book of Life. And the dead were judged according to their works, by the things which were written in the books.

What dead are these?

OK then, balls to the walls. God once spoke through a jackass. So here I will resort to inspired allegory to bray out scripture through the perception of His chosen *******. Afterwards, I'll provide scriptural support for heresies originally suggested by Origin himself.

For what seems to me to be too long a time, God has allowed Satan nearly free reign over our will. Just look at today's Trannie-Clown fest for example. Total madness reigns. Eventually this will lead to the international conflagration between the powers of the East versus the West commonly referred to as the Battle of Armageddon. That is in the valley of Megiddo where blood is prophesied to run as high as horse's bridles. Some of the imagery provided in biblical texts picture "giant locusts" resembling Apache War Choppers; Locusts with stingers and their tails spewing fire. Just imagine what ancient folks thought of that concept.

As the scripture warned. In those days, if they were not cut short by God, total nuclear annihilation would have been the end result. This was not the commonly understood style of war of the time using spears, swords, and the Roman phalanx. That fact provides further proof of the divine inspiration of these scriptures.

When this final battle begins God's church is in the depths of the final tribulation. This 'half-a-time' when Jesus returns announced by the shout of the Archangel and the blast of the trumpet. And Jesus takes hold of Satan and stops the madness. It is at this time that the dead in Christ have been raised from their graves and changed from fleshly to spiritual essence. Joining them in the clouds with the glorified Son are those still living at that moment in time. Then, united with Christ, they all return to Ground Zero to join in the task of fixing what centuries of misrule has fouled up.

One thing to note here is that the dead in Christ have been raised from their graves, not pulled out from heaven. Nor were they stuck back in their graves, into their old dead bodies for the sake of effect prior to being resurrected. Nowhere in scripture is heaven ever promised as the reward of the saved. It all becomes clear that, after Satan is bound in the pit, the Saints of Christ shall reign for 1000 years on earth over a world population intermixed with a combination of states still alive after Armageddon and God's Kingdom administered by the Saints.

After that. God releases Satan for a brief time so as to deceive the unconverted nations, who had not suffered Satan's deception for the thousand years of

God's Millennium, leading them into a final rebellion against God.

Why would God allow this? Well, that's all part of the plan, you see, so those few can learn the lesson already writ large in our present evil age. Maybe this was to be God giving Lucifer his final chance to repent. You'd think by now he would have figured that out and adjusted to the reality of the situation. Perhaps he's not actually permitted to do so. Maybe he's so under God's power that he lacks the free will to do other than that preordained by God. More likely this is because the nations who have known only God's rule through the millennium have yet to live through the Forbidden Fruit's lesson of the **knowledge of good versus evil**.

Either way, this attack doesn't go well for Satan, either. God rains down fire from heaven, consuming all the armies, grabbing Satan and tossing him and his minions into permanent lockdown in the bottomless pit.

Shortly following this another misunderstood event is mentioned. A second resurrection occurs, this time involving all the dead in human history. Everyone. Remember the first resurrection at the return of Christ only involved the dead in Jesus, his church, his followers. The rest of the dead, as is quoted, "lived not again until the thousand years was completed." At long last. Here is where the meat of God's overall plan becomes apparent. Imagine the massive world renovation going on at this time to prepare for the coming great population resurrection!

Before I wade into this, however, a few clarifications of language are required. Once in a lifetime, long, long ago, I visited the House of former President Harry S Truman in Independence, MO. On his desk was a placard stating his name. And rank. ***Judge Harry S Truman***.

Judge???

I wasn't aware he had earned a law degree. I was intrigued, not realizing he had been a judge.

I subsequently learned, however, that the term *judge* hasn't always meant what is thought of. It has another meaning, as opposed to someone like *Judge Judy*. Harry had no law degree. He did not judge the law. He was a county administrator of roads and other facilities. So, when we see Scripture referring to the Saints of God sitting in judgment of the remnant and recently resurrected, they are performing the same duties as was done in ancient Israel as related in the Biblical Book of Judges.

Ancient Israel, after the passing of Joshua until the reign of King Saul, was ruled by Judges, some good and some evil. "Thy rod and thy staff they comfort me" has to do with ruling and directing as we will be doing for the resurrected of the new Aeon. As for the books to be opened? Well, the Greek word for books comes from **biblios**, which is the same used for Bibles. So, the bibles will be opened, and the rule of God's kingdom will be administered from the teachings therein.

So, this vast population, which has never been able to understand or be taught the truth of God's way of give versus get, will finally be permitted to understand the lessons of our history written in the book of life. The fruits of obeying God versus what has happened as a result of disobeying God will be thoroughly absorbed.

The lesson of the forbidden fruit will now have been completed. The knowledge of good versus evil and all humanity, ALL HUMANITY: all religions, all populations, all nations will be free to accept or reject the free gift of God's grace. That has been God's plan all along since the beginning of time. And then glory of glories, in the next chapter of Revelation following these times, the Heavenly City of God will be established. It is pictured as coming down out of heaven to earth to replace the old physical universe.

There will no longer be day and night. It's referred to as The End of Days because time itself, as a physical construct, will cease to be. We've always looked at the term the end of days as being like the Viking Ragnarök when all things are destroyed. But it doesn't really mean that. It means this physical universe will no longer have substance and will be replaced by the spiritual: the Universal Kingdom of God.

Don't feel frustrated or confused. The whole concept is so beyond our limited understanding. Keep in mind God lives outside of time. Lives? Dwells? Who lives? That's not even a good term to apply for that. When Moses asked, who should I say sent me? God responded with, "Tell them I AM has sent you," because God simply IS! There is no before God. There is no after God. There is only God being God. So, it appears God just BE, and it has been written "so shall we be at that time." We cannot perceive what we will be, but when we see God as he is, we will understand because we will be the same.

All pain will be forgotten. All will be under grace. And should that concept annoy some, as we know it shall, they need to revisit the ***Parable of the Workers***

in the Field: Where some that had worked all day were upset that those who had joined in at the end of the day for a short time got the same reward. And don't forget, there's that ***Parable of the Prodigal Son*** who had left his father's house and run off to waste his inheritance before returning on his hands and knees to his father. His father welcomed him back and called for a great feast with the fatted calf and celebrated it; but his oldest son, who had remained faithful, was majorly pissed off because nothing like that had ever been done for him, and he had been faithful and doggone, "damned if old *Goody Two Shoes* was gonna take part in the celebration of it."

We don't know in Scripture if he ever did join in, but that initial caution against taking that sort of attitude remains "It's also been said about the self-righteous Pharisees "that, in the end, it will work out better for the population of Sodom and Gomorrah.

Sodom and Gomorrah!

The population of both cities will be there. And be forgiven by the grace of God. And the Pharisees no doubt will be upset about that, and it may cost but, but, we have done great works in your name, we've done this and we've done that."

And Jesus responded with, "Be gone, you nest of vipers. I never knew you. For you failed to show mercy on me in prison or naked or starving?"

When they cried out, "When did we do that to you?"

He said to them (and us) "when you did so to the least of my brethren, you did so also to me." So, Brothers. admonish one another to be happy. Be happy that God has concluded all in His embrace. And we, who endure to the end, shall be the first fruits setting the stage for what is to come. Consider all those poor souls who have suffered horror and death through the ages. Imagine healing them and opening their eyes to share in the Wonderful World of tomorrow's Kingdom of God. This has been God's grand plan all along. To save everyone. God, pray it be so and soon.

Revelation 21
A New Heaven and a New Earth

1 Then I saw "a new heaven and a new earth," for the first heaven and the first earth had passed away, and there was no longer any sea. **2** I saw the Holy City, the new Jerusalem, coming down out of heaven from God, prepared as a bride beautifully dressed for her husband. **3** And I heard a loud voice from the throne saying, "Look! God's dwelling place is now among the people, and he will dwell with them. They will be his people, and God himself will be with them and be their God. **4** 'He will wipe every tear from their eyes. There will be no more death' or mourning or crying or pain, for the old order of things has passed away." **5** He who was seated on the throne said, "I am making everything new!" Then he said, "Write this down, for these words are trustworthy and true." **6** He said to me: "It is done. I am the Alpha and the Omega, the Beginning and the End. To the thirsty I will give water without cost from the spring of the water of life. **7** Those who are victorious will inherit all this, and I will be their God and they will be my children.

Do not just skip over this and read on! Stop and consider how this changes everything. This is so momentous it seems such a message should be old news by now, but is it? Or is your mind having difficulty absorbing such a radical revelation? Think about it. How many questions has this singular work answered, from balancing the creation narrative, the nature of the Universe, and why God has allowed bad things to happen to good people? Consider all those basically nice people who couldn't justify faith in God with the contradictions of life as well as those societies who were totally invested in other creeds such as taught by the Dali Llama, Mohammed, Confucius, Ghandhi, or even Steven Hawking? What of the multitudes who lived and died prior to the Christian age? Isn't it a relief to, not only, know that God's Grace applies to them as well as you, but that He planned it all from the beginning to work out like that?

I am certain there will be any number of "but what abouts" brought up to counter what we have considered here. However, way back in the 3rd Century a great religionist expressed similar thoughts. As I have mentioned, Origen of Alexandria (c. 185–c. 253) was a leading teacher of his time and, through his writing, a powerful influence on the early church. His literary works laid a foundation for much thinking that followed. He was a Christian exegete who also made copious use of the allegorical method (the poetic moment). The allegorical method suggests that there is deeper meaning underneath the obvious literal text. It began with Greek philosophy and is foreign to the way people in the Old Testament generally interpreted Scripture leaving the exegete open to accusations of employing far-fetched, contradictory, and even heretical interpretations.

Although regularly running afoul of his ecclesiastical superiors, Origen was one of the most influential yet controversial figures in early Christian theology, apologetics, and asceticism. He has been described as "the greatest genius the early church ever produced." But I ask, how much of him or his teachings have we heard during church services? I've only recently learned of his existential teachings. I believe God would not hold me innocent were I to remain silent. I hope we all Get it now.

Theodore, Panegyric, a first-hand account of what listening to one of Origen's lectures in Caesarea was like:

It was like a spark falling in our deepest soul, setting it on fire, making it burst into flame within us. It was, at the same time, a love for the Holy Word, the most beautiful object of all that, by its ineffable beauty attracts all things to itself with irresistible force, and it was also love for this man, the friend and advocate of the Holy Word. I was thus persuaded to give up all other goals ... I had only one remaining object that I valued and longed for – philosophy, and that divine man who was my Master of Philosophy.

Origen believed that, eventually, the whole world would be converted to Christianity, "since the world is continually gaining possession of more souls." He believed that the Kingdom of Heaven was not yet come, but that it was the duty of every Christian to make the eschatological reality of the kingdom present in their lives. Origen is often believed to be a Universalist who suggested that all people might eventually attain salvation, but only after being purged of their sins through "divine fire." This, of course, in line of Origen's allegorical interpretation, was not *literal* fire, but rather the inner anguish of knowing one's own sins. Origen was also careful to maintain that universal salvation was merely a possibility and not a definitive doctrine.

Origen's conception of God the Father is apophatic—a perfect unity, invisible and incorporeal, transcending all things material, and therefore inconceivable and incomprehensible. He is likewise unchangeable and transcends space and time.

Origen is often seen as the first major Christian theologian. Though his orthodoxy had been questioned in Alexandria while he was alive, His faith eventually led to martyrdom.

Through this book his exegesis lives on.

POSTCRIPT

So, what is my main point in all this verbiage? First of all, I wanted to explore the freedom that comes with understanding how and why the collection of writings we refer to as the Bible is not all it's purported to be. Thereby that which we believe it implies may or may not necessarily be so. However, as in the Parables, it IS something from which God's Word can be gleaned if "rightly divided" with a mind unburdened with preconception. Remember Jesus stated He spoke in parables to hide the poetic moment from those unable to think beyond their limited grasp.

Those of us resistant to the 'leaven' of the Power Brokers and Gate Keepers of our society can be led by Jesus to see through the twisted web woven in support of their power. (Matt' 11:25) **"At that time Jesus answered and said, "I thank You, Father, Lord of heaven and earth, that You have hidden these things from the wise and prudent and have revealed them to babes."** I'm an example of how the Holy Spirit can open the eyes of an unwashed jackass to see what God has hidden from the ordained of Satan's world. A twisted take on the "Many are called, but few are chosen" could be "Many can see, but few are brave enough to open their eyes and raise their hands in challenge. How sad…

~~MY TAKE~~

So, here's the deal. It seems beyond obvious there have been multiple previous creations on our planet which the fossil record so proudly proclaims and for which holy scripture allows. Earth has been made use of as God's canvas wherein He has gone about the process of creating the resources, coal, oil, and other elements that the embryos of this latest womb can make use of. It is my view that Genesis 1:2-11 relates to a clean-up and reboot of the past world just prior to the "Garden of Eden account wherein YHVH began His plan of developing a superior god-kind developed in his own image. This process, which religionists have mistakenly referred to as "the fall," was simply a further step towards the ultimate goal.

With our metaphorical parents 'choosing' to bite into that fruit of the 'Knowledge of Good AND Evil' our species has ever after been writing a firsthand account of how every sort of lifestyle, but our Creator's Way of Give, results in. Having had foreknowledge of how this all would work out, YHVH **imbued** us all, NOT with Original Sin BUT, with Original Grace. That is the mystery of Grace which nobody seems to get. It IS a FREE GIFT! There are no preconditions; not even that we believe in Jesus. That would be of 'works,' and not a free gift. Satan, not God, is the accuser of the brethren. YHVH, our hug loving Father, has it all worked out for us.

The mass of humanity has been purposely blinded until the proper time for God's truth to be revealed. That is what all those resurrections mentioned at the conclusion of the *Apocalypse* are all about. First Jesus returns in power to end the final destructive conflagration putting Satan on a temporary time out so he can no longer stir the pot and mess up the new world ruling government. After that, the ultimate deceiver is allowed one last tantrum, drawing the still resistant nations into God's "ultimate classroom," after which the Deceiver is permanently dealt with. This is the point at which the most commonly mistaken resurrection takes place: "***The Great White Throne Judgement***" which is actually a period of administration, not condemnation.

<u>All</u> the dead throughout history, with the exception of those few who have already been glorified, are to be raised back to physical existence and judged. All of them! But not judged as we would commonly presume as with an old time Justice of the Peace. This judging has to do with administering society according to the Way of Jesus. The books (biblios) are to be opened teaching "The Way" as well as the "Book of Life;" a history of all that has occurred throughout the ages of human misrule (the history written under the shadow of that "Tree of the Knowledge of Good and Evil." THEN AND ONLY THEN, will all the human children have their truly first and only real opportunity to live according to the Gospel of the Kingdom of God.

There will be no eternal torture of sinners in hell-fire! Such a horror would not be representative of the loving God I have finally been led to know. Nor will an eternal retirement strumming harps in the clouds of heaven be the dubious "reward" of we whom YHVH has worked so masterfully at perfecting. Afterwards, once He has finished with Ragnarök, YHVH will **bring about the "end of night," and replace the present universe with a new creation wherein we will all dwell together in an eternal light and purpose yet to be revealed**.

That is the true *Gospel* (Good News) Jesus, the human Avatar of the Almighty Creator, came into our world proclaiming.

Please respond to me whether with torches and brickbats or questions and suggestions. However, this does bring up a question at this late date in our history. Why has this issue not been explored or even hinted at by the ordained, at least not since *Origen of Alexandria* back in the third century A.D? Do they have something to lose by discovering the actuality of Grace? I am encouraged by the few truth seekers I have tripped over on my journey. It is high time for those scorned believers in the Universal Grace of YHVH to stand tall and speak up.

I am reminded of my experience, related back in the 9th chapter, of preaching to the homeless street people at Chicago's *Pacific Garden Mission*. My mission had been to free them from the overriding concept they were beyond God's mercy with only eternal hell fire to look forward to. I was just finishing up about how they were all covered by grace – that God BE forgiving them, as I have already pointed out here, and that they needed only to forgive themselves and one another; when the resident preacher had jumped up waving his arms and crying out, "Enough, enough no more of this heresy!" He had then ordered me to shut up, leave the pulpit, and sit down!

So, what was it that had so offended that pastor? One would think he'd have been all for his lost boys to learn God had not forsaken them. But I guess, like the church in times past had delt with any contrary views, my clear heresy threatened his control. So, I have been terrified at how and why God has left this for me to reveal. Experience has informed me not to expect ecclesiastical praise. **Whatever** the cost, however, this revelation is too powerful to ignore. Pray for me.

W. F. Hauck Copyright 2023
billhauck41@gmail.com